The Snark Handbook

SEX EDITION

The Snark Handbook

SEX EDITION

INNUENDO, IRONY, AND ILL-ADVISED INSULTS ON INTIMACY

LAWRENCE DORFMAN

Skyhorse Publishing

Skyhorse Publishing books may be purchased in bulk at special discounts for sales promotion, corporate gifts, fund-raising, or educational purposes. Special editions can also be created to specifications. For details, contact the Special Sales Department, Skyhorse Publishing, 307 West 36th Street, 11th Floor, New York, NY 10018 or info@skyhorsepublishing.com.

Skyhorse® and Skyhorse Publishing® are registered trademarks of Skyhorse Publishing, Inc.®, a Delaware corporation.
www.skyhorsepublishing.com

10 9 8 7 6 5 4 3 2 1

Library of Congress Cataloging-in-Publication Data

Dorfman, Lawrence.
  The snark handbook : the sex edition : innuendo, irony, and ill-advised insults on intimacy / Lawrence Dorfman.
     p. cm.
  ISBN 978-1-61608-423-3 (alk. paper)
  1. Sex--Humor. 2. Sex--Quotations, maxims, etc. 3. Marriage--Humor. 4. Intimacy (Psychology)--Humor. I. Title.
  PN6231.S54D66 2011
  808.87--dc22
                              2011013936

Printed in China

Life without sex might be safer, but it would be unbearably dull. It is the sex instinct which makes women seem beautiful, which they are once in a blue moon, and men seem wise and brave, which they never are at all. Throttle it, denaturalize it, take it away—and human existence would be reduced to the prosaic, laborious, boresome, imbecile level of life in an anthill.

—HENRY LOUIS MENCKEN

Sex is the most fun you can have without laughing.

—WOODY ALLEN

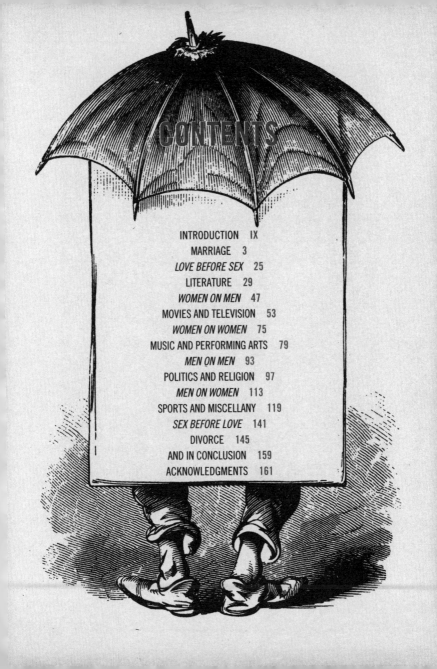

CONTENTS

INTRODUCTION   IX

MARRIAGE   3

LOVE BEFORE SEX   25

LITERATURE   29

WOMEN ON MEN   47

MOVIES AND TELEVISION   53

WOMEN ON WOMEN   75

MUSIC AND PERFORMING ARTS   79

MEN ON MEN   93

POLITICS AND RELIGION   97

MEN ON WOMEN   113

SPORTS AND MISCELLANY   119

SEX BEFORE LOVE   141

DIVORCE   145

AND IN CONCLUSION   159

ACKNOWLEDGMENTS   161

My sex life isn't dead but the buzzards are circling. ♦ What's "68"? You do m

Introduction

Sex can make you snarky. Snark can make you sexy.
—THE AUTHOR

AH YES . . . sex.

So much power for such a little word. We want it, we crave it, we need it, we hate it, we love it . . . are disgusted by it, attracted to it, appalled by it, enthralled by it . . . blah blah blah.

Just stop.

Try again.

Okay. Well, as you can see, it's pretty easy to get carried away when you indulge in the "sex" talk. For some reason, perhaps the fact that it's usually so closely associated with the L word (no, not the HBO series), we tend to romanticize sex . . . put it up on a pedestal . . . imbue it with power and mystery and intrigue and . . .

Yikes. There I go again.

This is getting out of hand. (Out of hand. Get it?)

I said stop!

Okay, okay…

S-E-X.

Sex can be great. Sex can be fun. Sex can be dirty (if you're doing it right). But most of all, sex can make you as snarky as the day is long. To paraphrase a corny eighties movie, you can go for weeks without sex, but try going even a day without a snark—just can't be done.

And I can't think of a better topic to make the snarks fly than sex, can you?

Whence It Came

Since that first moment when Adam said to Eve, "Stand back, I don't know how big this thing gets," sex has been an all-consuming endeavor for all of human kind. In fact, the image that starts this book was engraved in 1735 and describes a scene ripe for snark. It's part of an eight-painting series by artist William Hogarth titled *A Rake's Progress*. Know what a rake is? An immoral or dissolute person—in other words, someone who uses snark to the nth degree.

The first of the paintings (later turned into engravings) shows a young man named Tom Rakewell[1] after getting word of an unexpected windfall. He has dumped his pregnant fiancée (shown crying on the far right) and is being measured

---

[1]   Get it? Rake? Don't cha love it when those guys were so obvious?

for new duds. It's not a pretty picture, but as Bill Maher once said, "Men are only as loyal as their options."

Women, rejoice. He gets his comeuppance—he squanders his money on prostitutes and gambling and winds up insane. A result that members of both sexes can relate to.

We love sex. We love it, and it pisses us off, and occasionally it sends us to the loony bin. And, man, it's everywhere.

Today, sex is used to sell us useless shit. The brilliant Bill Hicks used to say that the perfect Coke ad would be a shot of a beautiful woman, scantily dressed. The camera would come in slowly as her two fingers of her right hand reached down between her legs. She would clearly be in the throes of an orgasm, or pretty close. As the camera close in on her face, she would look up and say two words: "Drink… Coke." And every male in America would be popping a can immediately (another euphemism?).

When sex and snark meet, watch out. Snark is a powerful tool… almost as powerful as sex .

What You Hold

So, what *is* this book then? Is it a slick guide to saying all the right things so you can score easily with the ladies/gents? No, of course not. Stick with fifties and hundreds.

Is it a crass self-help book that will make you feel good about your feeble attempts to procreate, to get off, to further

uring foreplay because there isn't time. • She looks like Olive Oyl's older, less

along your quest for making the *sex*? Crass, yes. Self-help? Not on your life.

This book is, quite frankly, a gathering of the finest minds, words, and thoughts of the great and near-great, the funny and the profane, the moronic and the majestic, the dirty and the dignified (will I ever stop?) in a quest to take advantage of a moment in time and make a few shekels off the puerile need to glorify the act—the act of making love, screwing, boffing, doing the in and out, bonking, making the two-back beast . . . well, you get the picture. (Now get the picture out of your head and keep reading.)

Categorizing the Deed

Let's face it, a man is a lot better than a woman at putting sex into a specific box in his mind.[2] Women always want to blur those lines—"how can you sleep with me and then not call me for three weeks?" Love and sex are not linked, ladies, and what's with the sleeping euphemism? If we're together, the LAST thing anyone's gonna be doin' is sleeping.

But I digress, yet again. All I'm trying to say is that for the sake of your reading pleasure, I have divided the book into various sections. As a man, I can do that. Compartmentalize. However, as a man who would like to keep having sex,

---

[2]   Ignore the double entendre.

I will also concede that they do occasionally overlap. It can get complicated.

What's It About Again??

So . . .

This is book filled with an interesting cast of sexual characters, some known, some unknown, but all with something snarky to say. Learn from them. There are sexy movie stars who are "married". . . . There are sexy lesbians who write books. There are sexy politicians[3] who fall in love and have sex, get married, have lots of sex without love, and ultimately are divorced. There are athletes who . . . well, sometimes people really are good at only one thing.

This is the third in the *Snark* series, and I think it's the funniest one yet. You'll laugh, you'll cry, you'll shake, you'll shudder, you'll . . . (see.. impossible to stop . . . just go with it, okay?). And often, at the same time, the hammer of recognition hits you squarely between your eyes.

But don't fret. After all, snark, like sex, is about survival. Embrace it and they can both set you free.

Enjoy—and stay snarky.

Lawrence Dorfman
September, 2011

---

[3]   Oxymoron?

lower than everyone else's.   •   He has all the sex appeal of a sweaty sock.   •   She's

AUTHOR'S NOTES

so cold she has her period in cubes. • If men had periods, they'd brag about t

1. There are bunch of quotes in here, a gaggle of jokes, some limericks, lots of one-liners, fun, games, fun and games. It's a snark book, after all. We found some great illustrations . . . even one that's rated R (see if you can find it)[4]. I got some reviews about my last book not being appropriate for certain ages. Ya think? Use your discretion and your judgment. And then decide if you want to let your parents read this. Or don't. Your call.

2. Similar to the second book, there's a smattering of pieces I call "Snarkin' the News," taken from the daily snarks on my Snark Handbook Facebook page. Mostly these are a commentary on how dumb humans are, but there's a lot of stuff on what I like to call "conjugating the verb[5]."

---

[4] Already looking, ain't cha?
[5] Being a faux-literary guy and all.

you could fax her. ♦ If sex were fast food, there'd be an arch over her bed. ♦ M

The Snark Handbook
SEX EDITION

HARMONY before MATRIMONY.

difference between pornography and erotica is lighting. • Sometimes I feel t

Marriage

"What is a marriage if not an opportunity to mock someone through thick and thin while simultaneously exploring your deepest, darkest, sexual desires?"
—MARCY RUNKLE, *CALIFORNICATION*

THEY SAY, "HOME IS where the heart is." Yes, that's mostly true, but home is also, more often, where the hard-on is. No place is as fertile a snark breeding ground as the institution of marriage (and who wants to be in an institution?). Think *The Hot Zone* minus those HazMat suits. It does, however, promise one thing: another body available for coupling.

It's been the same deal since James Gillray painted the caricature opposite, in 1805. Called "Harmony before Matrimony," it paints a foreboding portrait of marriage. Note the painting on the wall, with Cupid shooting a pair of doves. Or the cats fighting on the floor. There are even more negative elements, cropped in the interest of space. And Gillray

a lesbian trapped in a man's body—which actually works out pretty well for

followed up with an "after" painting. We'll get to that . . . in 140 pages. In the meantime, let's snark.

Getting married for sex is like buying a 747
for the free peanuts.
—JEFF FOXWORTHY

+++

A husband is what is left of a lover after the
nerve has been extracted.
—HELEN ROWLAND

++

Bachelors know more about women than
married men; if they didn't, they'd be married too.
—H. L. MENCKEN

+++

A man in love is incomplete until he is married.
Then he is finished.
—ZSA ZSA GABOR

++

Honeymoon: A short period of doting between
dating and debting.
—MIKE BINDER

me. • A little coitus never hoitus. • Marriage means commitment. Of course,

These days, the honeymoon is rehearsed
much more often than the wedding.
—P. J. O'ROURKE

~◆~

*A honeymoon couple goes to a hotel and asks
for a suite. "Bridal?" asks the desk clerk. "No
thanks," replies the bride, "I'll just hang on to
his shoulders."*

~◆~

Sex drive: a physical craving that begins
in adolescence and ends in marriage.

◆◆◆

I blame my mother for my poor sex life. All she told me
was "the man goes on top and the woman underneath." For
years, my husband and I slept in bunk beds.
—JOAN RIVERS

◆◆

Never get married in the morning, because
you never know who you'll meet that night.
—PAUL HORNUNG

◆◆◆

I came from a big family. As a matter of fact, I never got to
sleep alone until I was married.
—LEWIS GRIZZARD

Sexual Indiscretions Match Box[6]

A. John Edwards   D. Larry Craig

B. Amy Fisher   E. David Letterman

C. Marv Albert   F. Elizabeth Taylor

~•~

1. A sportscaster who became the butt of jokes when he was accused of sodomy and other bizarre sexual proclivities by a woman with whom he had a decade-long affair. His longtime girlfriend stood by him, and they recently married. That's what I call true love.

2. This movie star was married eight times to seven husbands. When her third husband died, she married his best friend (who was already married to someone else). They divorced; she married another film star whom she divorced, remarried, and divorced again. Two more to go[7].

3. A married senator, with a strong antigay platform, allegedly caught in an airport men's room using his foot to tap out sexual preferences to the FBI agent in the next stall. He says he was just picking up a piece of paper[8].

---

[6] 1. C, 2. F, 3. D, 4. B, 5. A, 6. E

[7] When you can't sleep, count her husbands.

[8] Yeah, a mash note.

4. A complete unknown, she entered into a love tryst at seventeen with a thirty-six-year-old married mechanic and then shot and seriously injured his wife. Also had a sex tape. Still unknown.

5. A strong family-values presidential candidate, he was the subject of a sex tape with his mistress, who was pregnant with his love child at the time. Meanwhile, his wife was dying of cancer. Whaddaya think of those values?

6. After being outed by a news staffer, this married television host and comedian confessed to finding his fun at the office through affairs with several members of his staff.

I never knew what real happiness was until
I got married. By then it was too late.
—MAX KAUFFMAN

••

The term "sex addict" makes it sound like
sex is a drug. And after 23 years of marriage,
in my house it's a controlled substance.
—BOBBY SLAYTON

•••

Before I married my husband, I'd never fallen in love,
although I'd stepped in it a few times.
—RITA RUDNER

~♦~

After twenty years of marriage, a couple was lying in bed one evening, when the woman felt her husband begin to fondle her in ways he hadn't in quite some time. It almost tickled as his fingers started at her neck and then began moving down past the small of her back. He then caressed her shoulders and neck, slowly worked his hand down over her breasts, stopping just over her lower stomach. He then proceeded to place his hand on her left inner arm, caressed past the side of her breast again, working down her side, passed gently over her buttock, and down her leg to her calf. Then, he proceeded up her inner thigh, stopping just at the uppermost portion of her leg. He continued in the same manner on her right side and then suddenly stopped, rolled over, and became silent. As she had become quite aroused by this caressing, she asked in a loving voice, "Honey, that was wonderful. Why did you stop?" "I found the remote."

~♦~

two-way treat. ♦ Bachelor: the only man who has never told his wife a lie. ♦ Hon

Husbands think we should know where everything is—
like the uterus is a tracking device. He asks me, "Do we
have any Cheerios left?" Like he can't go over to the
sofa cushion and lift it himself.
—ROSANNE BARR

••

How to Seduce Your Wife:

Compliment her, cuddle her, kiss her, caress her,
stroke her, tease her, comfort her, protect her, hug her,
hold her, wine and dine her, buy things for her, listen to
her, care for her, stand by her, support her, buy flowers
for her, go to the ends of the earth for her . . .

How to Seduce Your Husband:

Show up naked. Bring beer.

Marriage is like a bank account.
You put it in, you take it out, you lose interest.
—IRWIN COREY

oking: where many a man thinks his wife is. ◆ Contrary to popular belief, the

Marriage is an alliance entered into by a man
who can't sleep with the window shut, and a woman
who can't sleep with the window open.
—GEORGE BERNARD SHAW

✦✦✦

Marriage marks the end of many short follies—
being one long stupidity.
—FRIEDRICH NIETZSCHE[9]

✦✦

As I grow older and older
And totter towards the tomb,
I find that I care less and less
Who goes to bed with whom.
—DOROTHY L. SAYERS

✦✦✦

It destroys one's nerves to be amiable every
day to the same human being.
—BENJAMIN DISRAELI

✦✦

If you made a list of the reasons why any couple
got married, and another list of the reasons for
their divorce, you'd have a hell of a lot of overlapping.
—MIGNON MCLAUGHLIN

---

[9]   What happened to what doesn't kill me makes me stronger?

small bumps around a woman's nipple are not Braille for "suck here." ✦ Condom

Marriage

All marriages are happy. It's the living together afterward
that causes all the trouble.
—RAYMOND HULL

✦✦✦

Marriage ceremony: an incredible metaphysical sham of
watching God and the law being dragged into the affairs of
your family.
—O. C. OGILVIE

~✦~

*Robert Schimmel's wife told him about a hot
book about finding a woman's G-spot. "I went
to a bookstore. I couldn't even find the book."*

~✦~

That quiet mutual gaze of a trusting husband and
wife is like the first moment of rest or refuge
from a great weariness or a great danger.
—GEORGE ELIOT

✦✦

I hear love is entirely a matter of chemistry . . . must be why
my wife treats me like toxic waste.
—DAVID BISONETTE

re easier to change than diapers. ✦ The only thing wrong with wife-swapping is

In Pursuit of Sex, Men Will . . .

> ➤ GO SHOE SHOPPING—"No, they're very different than the seven other pairs in brown you looked at. I completely get the nuance of ecru."

> ➤ CLEAN THE BATHROOM—"I love the smell of Pine-Sol in the morning . . . smells like . . . cleanliness. And I will definitely put all three hundred of your products back where they were."

> ➤ WATCH THE NEIGHBOR'S KIDS—"Cool! Now I finally have a reason to watch six hours of *SpongeBob SquarePants* and *Veggie Tales*."

> ➤ EAT HEALTHY—"Yes, please bring me another helping of that spinach-kale-broccoli-asparagus salad shit, er . . . I mean, wow, tastes amazing!"

> ➤ THROW AWAY PICTURES OF OLD GIRL-FRIENDS—"No, babe, I threw those away. That box way up on that shelf in the garage that you can't reach is all the birthday cards you've sent me."

> ➤ WATCH A CHICK FLICK—"No, I really do think that Julia Roberts or Sandra Bullock or Natalie Portman *is* the modern-day Clint Eastwood. Love to go."

➢ HAVE DINNER AT HER MOTHER'S—"Of course, it's been too long since I examined every fault I have. I can play poker with the guys anytime."

➢ NOT LAUGH AT TASTELESS JOKES—"Not funny. After all, blondes have feelings too. I'm appalled."

➢ GO GROCERY SHOPPING—"Sure, I'll get your tampons and Midol. If I can't find the size box you need, I can always ask the clerk."

➢ DRESS UP TO GO OUT, EVEN THOUGH IT'S NOT A WEDDING OR A FUNERAL— "Yeah, this suit makes me feel great, babe. It's just like being back at work."

➢ WATCH JIMMY FALLON INSTEAD OF LETTERMAN—"I can totally see it now: he *is* cuter."

➢ ADMIT A MISTAKE—(Hey, let's not get carried away. After all, it's only sex . . . only sex . . . only . . .) "Totally my fault, hon. Won't happen again."

~✦~

Wife: Why don't you ever call out my name when we're making love?

Husband: Because I don't want to wake you.

~✦~

Love: A temporary insanity curable by marriage.

—AMBROSE BIERCE, *THE DEVIL'S DICTIONARY*

✦✦✦

Married life teaches one invaluable lesson: to think of things far enough ahead not to say them.

—JEFFERSON MACHAMER

✦✦

Early on, he let her know who is the boss. He looked her right in the eye and clearly said, "You're the boss."

—ANONYMOUS

✦✦✦

I bought my wife a sex manual but half the pages were missing. We went straight from foreplay to postnatal depression.

—BOB MONKHOUSE

✦✦

So heavy is the chain of wedlock that it needs two to carry it, and sometimes three.

—ALEXANDRE DUMAS[10]

---

[10] Whole new perspective on *The Three Musketeers, no?*

The total amount of undesired sex endured by women is probably greater in marriage than in prostitution.

—BERTRAND RUSSELL

✦✦✦

Women like silent men; they think they're listening.

—GEORGE CARLIN

~✦~

A husband was feeling horny one evening, but his wife pushed him away. "Sorry, honey, but I have a gynecologist's appointment in the morning, and I want to stay fresh." He nuzzled up to her again. "You don't have a dental appointment, do you?"

~✦~

I'd marry again if I found a man who had fifteen million dollars and would sign over half of it to me before the marriage . . . and guarantee he'd be dead within the year.

—BETTE DAVIS

✦✦

Marriage isn't all that it's cracked up to be. Let me tell you, honestly. Marriage is probably the chief cause of divorce.

—FRANK BURNS, *M·A·S·H*

> If variety is the spice of life, marriage is a big can
> of leftover Spam.
> —JOHNNY CARSON

◆◆◆

Snarkin' the News:

↪ A California scientist has invented a lipstick that turns bright crimson on the lips of the woman wearing it when she's in the mood for sex. But be careful. He gave one to his girlfriend, and when he came home, his wife wanted to know why all the blood was rushing to his head.

↪ A man went skinny-dipping on a beach in New Zealand. Afterward, he fell asleep on the beach. He was awakened by a poisonous spider biting his penis. It swelled to six times its normal size. Now he has the twelve inches his wife has always wanted.

↪ Two women teachers in South Carolina were arrested recently for having sex and drug parties with their students over the summer. Guess they were tired of reading boring "What I Did on My Summer Vacation" essays and wanted to spice things up.

can't hurt you unless you fall off. ◆ If you use the electric vibrator near water, yo

After ten years of marriage, being good in bed means you don't steal the covers.
—BRENDA DAVIDSON

++

Housework is like bad sex. Every time I do it, I swear I will never do it again. Until the next time company comes.
—MARILYN SOKOL

+++

The trouble with some women is that they get all excited about nothing—and then marry him.
—CHER

~+~

A father walks into his son's room and finds the boy pleasuring himself. He says, "Son, if you don't stop, you'll go blind!" "Dad, I'm over here!"

~+~

The reason for much matrimony is patrimony.
—OGDEN NASH

++

I got married, and we had a baby nine months and ten seconds later.
—JAYNE MANSFIELD

I come and go at the same time. • Women are like fine wine. They all start out

Things Not to Say During Sex

➤ You woke me up for that?

➤ Do you smell something burning?

➤ Try breathing through your nose.

➤ Can you please pass me the remote control?

➤ On second thought, let's turn off the lights.

➤ And to think—I was trying to pick up your friend!

While redecorating, I realized my wife and I have dramatically different tastes in furniture. She wanted to keep the pieces that reflected the French provincial theme she was creating; I wanted to keep the stuff we'd had sex on.

—BRAD OSBERG

~+~

A little boy gets up to go to the bathroom in the middle of the night. As he passes his parents' bedroom, he peeks in through the keyhole. He watches for a moment and then continues on down the hallway, saying to himself, "Boy, and she gets mad at me for sucking my thumb."

~+~

fresh, fruity, and intoxicating and then turn full-bodied with age until they go

Kids. They're not easy. But there has to be some
penalty for sex.
—BILL MAHER

~♦~

*A mother took her young daughter to the zoo.
When they reached the elephant enclosure, the
bull elephant looked angry and, to the embar-
rassment of the mother, had a huge erection.
"Do you think he'll charge?" asked the little girl.
"Well, I think he'd be entitled to," sighed her
mother.*

~♦~

Don't bother discussing sex with small children.
They rarely have anything to add.
—FRAN LEBOWITZ

♦♦♦

I believe in making the world safe for our children
but not our children's children, because I don't
think children should be having sex.
—JACK HANDEY

♦♦

There's only one way to have a happy marriage and as soon as
I learn what it is I'll get married again.
—CLINT EASTWOOD

ur and vinegary and give you a headache. ♦ Men are like a fine wine. They all

~•~

A couple has just had sex. The woman says, "If I got pregnant, what would we call the baby?" The man takes off his condom, ties it in a knot, and flushes it down the toilet. "Well, if he can get out of that, we'll call him Houdini."

~•~

Do you know what it means to come home to a little affection, a little tenderness, and a little sympathy? It means you're in the wrong house.

—JEFF FOXWORTHY

•••

The conception of two people living together for twenty-five years without having a cross word suggests a lack of spirit only to be admired in sheep.

—ALAN PATRICK HERBERT

••

I wonder, among all the tangles of this mortal coil, which one contains tighter knots to undo, and consequently suggests more tugging, and pain, and diversified elements of misery, than the marriage tie.

—EDITH WHARTON

•••

One man's folly is another man's wife.

—Helen Rowland

start out like grapes, and it's our job to stomp on them and keep them in the da

We were happily married for eight months. Unfortunately, we were married for four and a half years.

—NICK FALDO

••

In Hollywood a marriage is a success if it outlasts milk.

—RITA RUDNER

~•~

A man walks into the bedroom with a sheep under his arm. His wife is lying in bed, reading. "This is the pig I have sex with when you've got a headache," the man says. "I think you'll find that's a sheep," the wife says. "Yes, and I was talking to it, not you."

~•~

I know nothing about sex because I was always married.

—ZSA ZSA GABOR

•••

Remember, that if thou marry for beauty, thou bindest thyself all thy life for that which perchance will neither last nor please thee one year; and when thou hast it, it will be to thee of no price at all; for the desire dieth when it is attained, and the affection perisheth when it is satisfied.

—SIR WALTER RALEIGH[11]

---

[11] The man who gave us smokes after sex.

Such is the common process of marriage. A youth and maiden exchange meeting by chance, or brought together by artifice, exchange glances, reciprocate civilities, go home, and dream of one another. Having little to divert attention, or diversify thought, they find themselves uneasy when they are apart, and therefore conclude that they shall be happy together. They marry, and discover what nothing but voluntary blindness had before concealed; they wear out life in altercations, and charge nature with cruelty.

—SAMUEL JOHNSON

✦✦

American women expect to find in their husbands a perfection that English women only hope to find in their butlers.

—W. SOMERSET MAUGHAM

~✦~

Q. *What is the difference between a bachelor and a married man?*

A. *Bachelor comes home, sees what's in the refrigerator, goes to bed. Married man comes home, sees what's in the bed, and goes to the refrigerator.*

~✦~

Snarkin' the Facts

> ➤ *Historical records show that even in 1850 BC, women attempted to practice birth control. The most common method was a mixture of crocodile dung and honey placed in the vagina in the hopes of preventing pregnancy. But the absolute best method of birth control was getting the man to collect the crocodile dung.*

> ➤ *The vibrator, a common sex toy for women, was originally designed in the nineteenth century as a medication to combat the anxiety-related symptoms of hysteria. There were batteries in the nineteenth century? Or did they just need to hire someone to shake them real fast?*

> ➤ *According to Alfred Kinsey's Sexual Behavior in the Human Male, 81 percent of men say they have experienced nocturnal emissions. "Honey, I know I was calling my assistant's name, but it was you I was dreaming about, dressed as my assistant—I swear."*

> ➤ *Worldwide, sexually active adults report having sex an average of 103 times per year. That's twice a week. Given the law of averages, somebody's not ever getting out of bed.*

Things NOT to say at a wedding

1. Hey, I think I saw that same dress at Costco!
2. What's the over/under on whether this one will take?
3. Gonna be some ugly kids, no?
4. Get a load of the brides/groom's mom . . . Thanksgiving's gonna be a hoot.
5. I hope they love the vibrator I gave them.
6. Who catered this, Taco Bell?
7. Hopefully there'll be his and her bathrooms and his won't have any mirrors.
8. It's a fairytale wedding - and her mom get's to be the ogre.
9. Is that a bump Maybe we need to throw puffed rice.
10. His marriage vows will be silence and poverty.
11. It's not that he's going to live longer, it's just going to seem longer.
12. You know how many hookers he could have had for what this wedding costs?
13. What a fastidious couple. She's fast and he's hideous.

My wife and I were happy for twenty years. Then we met.
—RODNEY DANGERFIELD

before or after, but instead. ◆ The difference between light and hard is that yo

LOVE
BEFORE
SEX

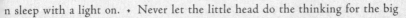

n sleep with a light on. ⋅ Never let the little head do the thinking for the big

LOVE BEFORE SEX

"First comes *love*, then comes *marriage* . . ?" What's the next line? Ah, yes: "Then comes baby in the baby carriage." Now if that doesn't make your toes curl, you're reading the wrong book. Sure, the idea of love before sex is lovely, if antiquated. I'll bet you think that you'll still love your spouse when he or she is 93. You won't even notice how large those underpants are getting—that is, when you actually have a chance to peer into the great canyon that once smartly connected two halves of a tight ass. Even your granny will tell you that falling in love blinds you; that having sex while blind may heighten your sensations[12]; and that heightened sensations lead to marriage, which leads to a baby in a baby carriage. 'Nuf said.

Love is an electric blanket with somebody else in control of the switch.[13]
—CATHY CARLYLE

My wife is pregnant—she took seriously what was poked at her in fun.

✦

Love and eggs are best when fresh.

My wife wants Olympic sex — every four years.

✦

My wife only has sex with me for a purpose. Last night it was to time an egg.

---

[12] Stay with me. There's a point here, somewhere.

[13] It's why love never survives outdoor in the rain.

head. ✦ My wife says I never listen to her. At least I think that's what sl

Love is blind but marriage is a real eye-opener.

♦

Love, the quest; marriage, the conquest; divorce, the inquest.

♦

Her kisses left something to be desired—the rest of her.

Marry at 20 and you'll be shocked at who you're living with at 30.

♦

Love is only a dirty trick played on us to achieve continuation of the species.
—W. SOMERSET MAUGHAM

By all means marry; if you get a good wife, you'll be happy. If you get a bad one, you'll become a philosopher.
—SOCRATES

♦

Love at first sight is one of the greatest labor-saving devices the world has ever seen.

Romantic love is . . . a drug. It distorts reality, and that's the point of it. It would be impossible to fall in love with someone you really saw.
—FRAN LEBOWITZ

Until I got married, I was my own worst enemy.

the way, why go at all? • I am a man of few words and a thousand obscer

Literature

Home is heaven and orgies are vile
But you need an orgy, once in a while.
—OGDEN NASH

THROUGH THE AGES, THOSE that put chisel to stone, pen to paper, or fingers to keyboard have had much to say, good and bad, about the S-word. One could argue that many start writing to get the opposite sex to pay attention to them.[14] Or to live vicariously through the lives of sensual, erotic characters . . . to feel the hands of a lover . . . to imagine the pounding of a horse's hooves . . . to "graze on my lips; and if those hills be dry, stray lower, where the pleasant fountains lie."[15] I will leave it to the great to provide for the less great. Go ahead, borrow at will...or from Will, for that matter.

---

[14] Works like a charm. Really. No, really.
[15] Oh you snarky bard-ster.

Everything in the world is about sex except sex.
Sex is about power.
—OSCAR WILDE

+++

It's all this cold-hearted fucking that is death and idiocy.
—D. H. LAWRENCE

++

The kiss is a wordless articulation of desire whose
object lies in the future, and somewhat to the south.
—LANCE MORROW

+++

There once was a sailor from Brighton
Who said to a lass, "You're a tight one."
She said, "Pon my soul, you're in the wrong hole!
There's plenty of room in the right one."

++

Sex is as important as eating or drinking, and we ought to
allow the one appetite to be satisfied with as little restraint
or false modesty as possible.
—MARQUIS DE SADE

+++

Never accept rides from strange men, and remember
that all men are strange as hell.
—ROBIN MORGAN

were outlawed, only outlaws would have in-laws. • Masturbation is l

Dorothy Parker

↝ You can lead a horticulture, but you can't make her think.

↝ His voice was as intimate as the rustle of bedsheets.

↝ Brevity is the soul of lingerie.

↝ One more drink and I'd be under the host.

↝ Tell him I've been too fucking busy—or vice versa.

↝ Ducking for apples—change one letter and it's the story of my life.

Girls who put out are tramps. Girls who don't are ladies. This is, however, a rather archaic usage of the word. Should one of you boys happen upon a girl who doesn't put out, do not jump to the conclusion that you have found a lady. What you have probably found is a lesbian.
—FRAN LEBOWITZ

♦♦

How horny can you get? I don't know, what's the record?
—NEIL SIMON

For once you must try not to shirk the facts
Man is kept alive by bestial acts.
—BERTOLT BRECHT

✦✦✦

My own belief is that there is hardly anyone whose sexual
life, if it were broadcast, would not fill the world at large
with surprise and horror.
—W. SOMERSET MAUGHAM

✦✦

The first kiss is magic, the second is intimate, the third is
routine. After that you just take the girl's clothes off.
—RAYMOND CHANDLER

✦✦✦

A man must hug, and dandle, and kistle, and play a hundred
little tricks with his bed-fellow when he is disposed to make
that use of her that nature designed her for.
—DESIDERIUS ERASMUS

✦✦

A woman tries to get all she can out of a man, and a man
tries to get all he can into a woman.
—ISAAC GOLDBERG

✦✦✦

The happiness of a man in this life does not consist in the
absence but in the mastery of his passions.
—ALFRED LORD TENNYSON

True or False?

- ↪ Masturbate is used to catch large fish.
- ↪ A dildo is a variety of sweet pickle.
- ↪ Ovaries are a French egg dish made with cheese.

Nothing in our culture, not even home computers, is more
overrated than the epidermal felicity of two featherless
bipeds in desperate congress.

—QUENTIN CRISP

++

Leaving sex to the feminists is like letting your
dog vacation at the taxidermist.

—CAMILLE PAGLIA

+++

All this fuss about sleeping together . . . for physical pleasure
I'd sooner go to my dentist any day.

—EVELYN WAUGH

++

It is with our passions, as it is with fire and water, they are
good servants but bad masters.

—AESOP

Sex Is . . .

➢ Sex is like death, only after death you don't feel like a pizza.
>   —WOODY ALLEN

✦✦✦

➢ Sex is like art. Most of it is pretty bad, and the good stuff is out of your price range.
>   —SCOTT ROEBEN

✦✦

➢ Sex is like money. Only too much is enough.
>   —JOHN UPDIKE

✦✦✦

➢ Sex is kicking death in the ass while singing.
>   —CHARLES BUKOWSKI

✦✦

➢ Sex is a beautiful thing between two people. Between five, it's fantastic.
>   —WOODY ALLEN

✦✦✦

➢ Sex is conversation carried out by other means.
>   —PETER USTINOV

✦✦

➢ Sex is. There's nothing to be done about it.
>   —ANONYMOUS

won't either. ✦ An erection is like the Theory of Relativity - the more you thi

Sex builds no roads, writes no novels, and sex certainly gives
no meaning to anything in life but itself.
—GORE VIDAL

✦✦✦

Money, it turned out, was exactly like sex, you
thought of nothing else if you didn't have it and
thought of other things if you did.
—JAMES BALDWIN

✦✦

People don't think of writers as sex objects.
The women who write to me and suggest that we
ought to have sex usually turn out to be, like, eighty.
And their letters always end with, "Just joking."[16]
—DAVE BARRY

✦✦✦

She gave me a smile I could feel in my hip pocket.
—RAYMOND CHANDLER

✦✦

Tantric sex is very slow. My favorite position is
the *plumber*. You stay in all day and nobody comes.
—JOHN MORTIMER

---

[16] No, really.

Things Not to Say During Sex

➤ Well, so much for mouth-to-mouth.

➤ Hope you're as good looking when I'm sober . . .

➤ Do you get any premium movie channels?

➤ Try not to smear my makeup . . .

➤ Got any penicillin?

➤ I thought you had the keys to the handcuffs!

For flavor, instant sex will never supersede the
stuff you have to peel and cook.
—QUENTIN CRISP

✦✦✦

When they circumcised him, they threw away the wrong bit.
—DAVID LLOYD GEORGE

✦✦

I bought a condom, and put it in my wallet when I was
fourteen. By the time I pulled it out to use it, it was older
than the girl I was with.
—LEWIS GRIZZARD

~+~

The late Truman Capote was in a New York restaurant on one of those rare nights that found him both sober and not drugged. He was instantly recognized, and a succession of female admirers came across to his table to laud his work and offer matchbooks and paper napkins for him to sign. The husband of one of them objected that such feminine emotion should be wasted on a self-confessed homosexual. He leaned across the table, unzipped his fly, and hung his penis out under Capote's nose. "Maybe you'd like to sign this," he suggested. Capote inspected the dangling member politely. "I don't know if I can sign it," he said. "Maybe I could just initial it."

~+~

One of the principal differences between a woman and a volcano is that a volcano can't fake eruptions.

—TIM DEDOPULOS

+++

Sex is interesting, but it's not totally important. I mean, it's not even as important (physically) as excretion. A man can go seventy years without a piece of ass, but he can die in a week without a bowel movement.

—CHARLES BUKOWSKI

...er word that needs some good old - fashioned four-letter words in order to

Snarkin' the News

↔ Sexting is hot. Women prefer Facebook, but men are more partial to Twitter because you only need 140 characters, can smoke a virtual cigarette after, and then play video games.

↔ A major newspaper reported that a janitor discovered two female language teachers going at it hot and heavy in a Brooklyn school recently. That's not journalism; it's a letter to *Penthouse*.

↔ New on the market: porn for the blind. A Canadian photographer has created the first book of nudes in Braille . . . it's a popup, of course. It retails for $225. Hey, for that price . . .

The brain is viewed as an appendage of the genital glands.
—CARL JUNG

✦✦

An erection at will is the moral equivalent
of a valid credit card.
—ALEX COMFORT

You sleep with a guy once, and before you know it,
he wants to take you to dinner.
—MYERS YORI

✦✦✦

Don't have sex, man. It leads to kissing, and pretty soon
you'll have to start talking to them.
—STEVE MARTIN

✦✦

In the case of some women, orgasms take quite a bit of time.
Before signing on with such a partner, make sure you are
willing to lay aside, say, the month of June, with sandwiches
having to be brought in.
—BRUCE JAY FRIEDMAN

✦✦✦

If I were asked, "What makes a woman good in bed?" I
would answer, "A man who is good in bed."
—BOB GUCCIONE

✦✦

The only way Hugh Hefner can get stiff now
is through rigor mortis.
—GILBERT GOTTFRIED

✦✦✦

There's nothing inherently dirty about sex, but if you try real
hard and use your imagination, you can overcome that.
—LEWIS GRIZZARD

In my sex fantasy, nobody ever loves me for my mind.
—NORA EPHRON

••

Snarkin' the Facts

> More women talk dirty than men, according to Playboy magazine. And always to the pool boy or the TV repairman, according to Penthouse.

> Use of the condom was first noted in published literature in the early 1500s. The device was originally made of linen, and historians believe the legendary lover Casanova used linen condoms. It's why everyone was oh–so–careful whenever they were invited to a dinner party.

> Having a PhD makes a woman twice as likely to be interested in a one-night stand as her bachelor degree–holding counterparts. Most universities don't even cover casual sex until the master's programs.

As a young man, I used to have four supple members and one stiff one. Now I have four stiff and one supple.
—HENRI, DUC D'AUMALE

Even if you gods, and all the goddesses too, should
be looking on, yet would I be glad to sleep
with golden Aphrodite.

—HOMER[17]

✦✦✦

It is an infantile superstition of the human spirit that
virginity would be thought a virtue and not the barrier that
separates ignorance from knowledge.

—VOLTAIRE

✦✦

Niagara Falls is the bride's second great disappointment.

—OSCAR WILDE

✦✦✦

Of the delights of this world, man cares most for sexual
intercourse, yet he has left it out of his heaven.

—MARK TWAIN

✦✦

They're putting the cart before the horse on this
pornography issue. *Playboy* doesn't cause sexual thoughts.
Sexual thoughts exist, and, therefore, there is *Playboy*. Do
you see? I'm gonna clear the air for you tonight . . . Here's
what causes sexual thoughts: having a dick.

—BILL HICKS

---

[17] Winning!

stalled a handrail around the bed. ✦ Sects! Sects! Sects! Is that all Monks think

I haven't trusted polls since I read that 62 percent of women had affairs during their lunch hour. I've never met a woman in my life that would give up lunch for sex.
—ERMA BOMBECK

+++

Oh, life is a glorious cycle of song,
A medley of extemporanea;
And love is a thing that can never go wrong;
And I am Marie of Romania.
—DOROTHY PARKER

++

Mortal lovers must not try to remain at the first step; for lasting passion is the dream of a harlot and from it we wake in despair.
—C. S. LEWIS

+++

Desperate is not a sexual preference.
—RANDY K. MILHOLLAND

++

Coition is a slight attack of apoplexy. For man gushes forth from man, and is separated by being torn apart with a kind of blow.
—DEMOCRITUS

Love ain't nothing but sex misspelled.
—HARLAN ELLISON

✦✦✦

William Shakespeare

- ↪ Is it not strange that desire should so many years outlive performance?

- ↪ Were kisses all the joys in bed, One woman would another wed.

- ↪ All lovers swear more performance than they are able.

- ↪ Can one desire too much of a good thing?

- ↪ Drink, sir, is a great provoker of three things . . . nose-painting, sleep, and urine. Lechery, sir, it provokes, and unprovokes; it provokes the desire, but it takes away the performance.

orse. He couldn't have done better and she couldn't have done worse. ✦ The sex

What Shakespeare Really Meant[18]

↝ Self-love, my liege, is not so vile a sin, as self-neglecting.
Translation: We should masturbate more.

↝ Be to yourself as you would to your friend.
Translation: It's OK to sleep with your sister because your friend sure would.

↝ Have patience, and endure.
Translation: Use one of those numbing creams if you have to. Or try wearing five condoms at once.

↝ They that thrive well take counsel of their friends.
Translation: If your drinking buddies say she's really a man, listen to them.

↝ That man that hath a tongue, I say, is no man, if with his tongue he cannot win a woman.
Translation: If you're desperate to impress her, you can always resort to oral sex.

↝ O, flatter me, for love delights in praises.
Translation: Honesty isn't necessarily the best policy when it comes to penis size.

---

[18] Reprinted with permission from Scott Roeben.

↝ Praising what is lost, makes the remembrance dear.
Translation: When you're telling your buddies about your conquests, exaggerate. A lot.

↝ My endeavors have ever come too short of my desires.
Translation: You've never had twins and you never will. Get over it.

Las Vegas is a society of armed masturbators / gambling is the kicker here / sex is extra / weird trip for high rollers . . . house-whores for winners / hand jobs for the bad luck crowd.
—HUNTER THOMPSON

✦✦

I have always thought that candy is the sex of childhood. It's the thing you think about a lot, because you aren't allowed to have it. It's replaced by sex in your adolescence. The same kind of plotting, secretiveness, the same kind of parental disapproval. And then you get to an age where you would just as soon have candy again.[19]
—FRANZ LEBOWITZ

---

[19] I'm partial to Mounds, myself.

~✦~

Josh: "What is this thing?"
Gasper: "It's a Yeti. An abominable snowman."
Biff: "This is what happens when you fuck a sheep?"
Josh: "Not an abomination, abominable."
—CHRISTOPHER MOORE

~✦~

I'm a heroine addict. I need to have sex with women who have saved someone's life.
—MITCH HEDBERG

each other a blow job. ✦ He's hung like Einstein and smart as a horse. ✦ It's lik

WOMEN ON MEN

...is, only smaller. ◆ Without nipples, breasts would be pointless. ◆ Her legs are

WOMEN ON MEN

When you think about the relationship between men and women, it's amazing that more men aren't killed in their sleep. Women deserve a medal for putting up with all the foibles, failings, and folderol that is truly at the heart of those creatures known as Homo hominis. We cheat, lie, flirt, cavort, leave the seat up, forget to call, forget to text . . . up to the minute that sex is involved. Then we find we have the memory of an elephant. Women communicate differently than men, cutting through the haze to get to the meat of the matter. Their brains are bigger, they react to stress better . . . but, like men, need to blow off steam regularly. Snark is the perfect tool. The following are examples of the steam that's shot out in the past. Careful . . . don't get burned.

I married beneath me. All women do.

—NANCY ASTOR

That useless piece of flesh at the end of a penis is a man.

—JO BRAND

When I think of the men I've slept with—if they were women—I wouldn't even have lunch with them.

—CAROL SUSSKIND

The difference between savings bonds and men? At some point, the bonds mature.

+

Springtime reminds me of the ex. Especially when I'm pruning out the dead wood.

+

If your husband and a lawyer were drowning and you had to choose, would you go to lunch or to a movie?

I'm not your type. I'm not inflatable.

+

Women have their faults. Men have only two: Everything they say. Everything they do.

We have a reason to believe that man first walked upright to free his hands for masturbation.

—LILY TOMLIN

Adam came first . . . but then, men always do.

Not all men are annoying. Some are dead.

Sex is like snow, you never know how many inches you're going to get or how long it will last.

Jesus was a typical man. They always say they'll come back, but you never see them again.

What do men and mascara have in common? They both run at the first sign of emotion.

Men and women, women and men. It will never work.

—ERICA JONG

A ring around the finger does not cause a nerve block to the genitals.

If vibrators could light the barbecue or kill spiders in the bathtub, would we need men at all?

—KATHY LETTE

doesn't have a dirty mind . . . he has introspective pornographic moments.   ◆   Co

Let'snotcomplicateourrelationship bytryingtocommunicatewitheach other.

⁘

Oral sex is like being attacked by a giant snail.

—GERMAINE GREER

⁘

If you want to sacrifice the admiration of many men for the criticism of one, go ahead, get married.

—KATHARINE HEPBURN

Love isn't blind, it's retarded.

⁘

To marry once is a duty; twice a folly; thrice is madness.

MARRIAGE IS A ROMANCE IN WHICH THE HEROINE DIES IN THE FIRST CHAPTER.

—CECILIA EGAN

He is every other inch a gentleman.

—REBECCA WEST

nkers have sex more frequently and enjoy it more than non-coffee drinkers. (Of

course, it all depends on whether your partner is Grande or Venti . . . and n

Movies and Television

Sex is more exciting on the screen and between
the pages than between the sheets.
—ANDY WARHOL

I HATE SEX IN THE movies. Tried it once . . . the seat folded up, the drink spilled, and the ice meited. Talk about chilling a mood . . .

Screen sex interrupts the action and takes you out of the moment. Yeah, I'm sure that_____(fill in your favorite movie star) would take a break from jumping over rooftops, kung fu-ing anything that moves, and shooting his way through windows if he had an opportunity to slip it to _____(fill in your other favorite movie star). No doubt in my mind.

Basically, sex is there to sell the single from the insipid soundtrack.

On TV, until recently, there was only the suggestion of sex. Married couples had separate beds, no one ever touched each other, and the moment there was the slightest indication that the scene was going past any more banal dialogue—cut to commercial! Until *NYPD Blue*, where we were treated to sex and nudity and all kinds of adult pursuits. Unfortunately, much of the ass we saw belonged to David Caruso or Dennis Franz: a far cry from Rob and Laura Petrie sleeping in separate beds, but still enough to put you off your dinner.

The best sex in either medium is the kind that's couched in witty barbs and top-of-the-line snark. Have a look.

Remember, sex is like a Chinese dinner.
It ain't over 'til you both get your cookie.
—ALEC BALDWIN

~•~

In a famous Letterman show exchange, Dr. Ruth Westheimer, the sex expert, included cucumbers in a list of handy sex objects for women. The next night, guest Ted Koppel asked, "May I insert something here?" "OK, as long as it's not a cucumber," responded David Letterman.

~•~

I was so flat, I used to put Xs on my chest
and write, "You are here."
—JOAN RIVERS

can't be trusted: he's fishier than Lady Godiva's saddle. • This gum tastes funny

~+~

Lucille: (holding her rape horn in one hand and a fireplace poker in the other) But I have a surprise for whoever it is if he comes back. First, I blow him, and then I poke him.
Michael: Guy has no idea what he's in for.

—ARRESTED DEVELOPMENT

~+~

Sex can be fun after eighty, after ninety, and after lunch.

—GEORGE BURNS

✦✦✦

The legs aren't so beautiful. I just know
what to do with them.

—MARLENE DIETRICH

✦✦

I appreciate this whole seduction thing you've got going on
here, but let me give you a tip: I'm a sure thing.

—PRETTY WOMAN

✦✦✦

I could never be a woman, 'cause I'd just stay home
and play with my breasts all day.

—LA STORY

Things Not to Say During Sex

- ➤ I wish we got the *Playboy* channel . . .

- ➤ But my cat always sleeps on that pillow

- ➤ Did I tell you my aunt died in this bed?

- ➤ No, really . . . I do this part better myself!

- ➤ It's nice being in bed with a woman I don't have to inflate!

- ➤ This would be more fun with a few more people . . .

Some things are better than sex, some things
are worse, but there's nothing exactly like it.
—W. C. FIELDS

♦♦

I'm trisexual—I'll try anything once.
— SAMANTHA, *SEX AND THE CITY*

♦♦♦

It's true that all men are pigs. The trick is to tame the one
who knows how to find truffles.
—LEV L. SPIRO

Woody Allen

- Remember, if you smoke after sex, you're doing it too fast.

- If there is reincarnation, I'd like to come back as Warren Beatty's fingertips.

- My brain is my second favorite organ.

- I'm such a good lover because I practice a lot on my own.

- I was involved in an extremely good example of oral contraception two weeks ago. I asked a girl to go to bed with me, and she said no.

- My wife and I thought we were in love, but it turned out to be benign.

- Sex between a man and a woman can be wonderful, provided you get between the right man and the right woman.

- I sold the memoirs of my sex life to a publisher. They're going to make a board game out of it.

- I think people should mate for life, like pigeons or Catholics.

er intercourse? Less competitive. • I was married once. Now I just lease. • I'm

A hooker once told me she had a headache.
—RODNEY DANGERFIELD

✦✦

Don't have sex, because you will get pregnant. And die. Don't have sex in the missionary position, don't have sex standing up, just don't do it, OK? Promise? OK, now everybody take some rubbers.
— COACH CARR, *MEAN GIRLS*

✦✦✦

Money is power; sex is power . . . therefore getting money for sex is simply an exchange of power.
—SAMANTHA, *SEX AND THE CITY*

✦✦

Sex education may be a good idea in the schools, but I don't believe the kids should be given homework.
—BILL COSBY

~✦~

Mrs. Teasdale: Oh, Your Excellency!
Firefly: You're not so bad yourself.
—*DUCK SOUP*

~✦~

I want a man who is kind and understanding. Is that too much to ask for in a millionaire?
—ZSA ZSA GABOR

not a breast man, I'm a breast person. ✦ Monogamous and monotono

~✦~

Elaine: I've yada yada'd sex.
George: Really?
Elaine: Yeah. I met this lawyer, we went out to dinner, I had the lobster bisque, we went back to my place, yada yada yada, I never heard from him again.
Jerry: But you yada yada'd over the best part.
Elaine: No, I mentioned the bisque.

—SEINFELD

~✦~

Now I know what I've been faking all these years.

—PRIVATE BENJAMIN

✦✦✦

You know when you hear girls say, "I was so shit-faced last night, I shouldn't have fucked that guy?" We could be that mistake!

—SUPERBAD

✦✦

I'm too shy to express my sexual needs except over the phone to people I don't know.

—GARRY SHANDLING

Groucho Marx

> ➤ Whoever called it necking was a poor judge of anatomy.

> ➤ Marry me and I'll never look at another horse!

> ➤ I chased a girl for two years only to discover that her tastes were exactly like mine: we were both crazy about girls.

> ➤ I remember the first time I had sex—I kept the receipt.

> ➤ I was married by a judge . . . I should have asked for a jury.

> ➤ I read so many bad things about sex that I had to give up reading.

The important thing in acting is to be able to laugh and cry. If I have to cry, I think of my sex life. If I have to laugh, I think of my sex life.
—GLENDA JACKSON

competitive. ◆ Pizza is a lot like sex. When it's good, it's really good. When it's ba

What's the difference between sex and love? I have four wives and five kids. I apparently don't know the difference.
—JAMES CAAN

✦✦✦

Women are the quickest to call other women sluts, which is sad. I haven't met a lot of men who've said, "You like having sex? What a dirty whore you are!" That's because they wish their wives or girlfriends would have more sex with them.
—MEGAN FOX

~✦~

Ben: Do you want to do it doggy style?
Alison: You're not going to fuck me like a dog.
Ben: It's doggie style. It's just the style. We don't have to go outside or anything.
—*KNOCKED UP*

~✦~

I'll come and make love to you at five o'clock. If I'm late, start without me.
—TALLULAH BANKHEAD

✦✦

Masturbation is nothing to be ashamed of. It's nothing to be particularly proud of, either.
—MATT GROENING

✦✦✦

still pretty good. ✦ Hypocrite: Someone who complains that there is too much

~•~

The famously well-endowed Jayne Mansfield often "accidentally" upstaged other actresses with her remarkable breasts. On one occasion, Mansfield "bent over" at a Hollywood reception for Sophia Loren, and one of her ample breasts tumbled out of her dress. Actor Clifton Webb was sitting beside Sophia when Jayne leaned in. "Please, Ms. Mansfield," he remarked, "we're wine drinkers at this table."

~•~

There was a young lady named Iair
Who possessed a magnificent pair,
Or at least so I thought
Till I saw one get caught
on a thorn and begin losing air.

••

It's like sex with an orgasm at the end of it. Whereas film is like you have sex but you never get the orgasm. A lot of stopping and starting.
—KIERA KNIGHTLY (ON STAGE ACTING)

•••

Pussy: My name is Pussy Galore.
Bond: I must be dreaming.
—GOLDFINGER

~♦~

David Letterman: I think sex on the first date is . . .?

Jessica Alba: Fine . . .

David Letterman: Fine. You said that sort of unenthusiastically, like, fine, getting a good parking place.

Jessica Alba: Sometimes a good parking place is better.

~♦~

Hell, if I'd jumped on all the dames I'm supposed to have jumped on, I'd have had no time to go fishing.

—CLARK GABLE

♦♦

I wasn't being free with my hands—
I was trying to guess her weight.

—W. C. FIELDS

~♦~

Niles: Are you quite finished undressing him with your eyes?

Roz: Oh please, I'm already looking for my stockings and trying to remember where I parked my car.

—FRASIER

~♦~

a sexually transmitted disease. ♦ Sex is a conversation carried out by other

Match the Sex Snark to the Celebrity[20]

A. Ben Affleck
B. Jennifer Aniston
C. Johnny Depp
D. Megan Fox

E. Angelina Jolie
F. Marilyn Monroe
G. Brad Pitt
H. Julia Roberts

~✦~

1. I'm so tired of being part of this sick, twisted Bermuda Triangle.
2. I hate the whole reluctant sex-symbol thing. It's such bull. You see these dudes greased up, in their underwear, talking about how they don't want to be a sex symbol.
3. The fact is I am not having sex. But I feel absolutely ripe for the, what would you say . . . plucking?
4. Being married means I can break wind and eat ice cream in bed.
5. The only gossip I'm interested in is things from the *Weekly World News*—"Woman's Bra Bursts, 11 Injured." That kind of thing.
6. Sex is a part of nature. I go along with nature.
7. I really enjoy having sex, and that's offensive to some people.
8. I've never had to pretend to be having sex with somebody. I'm like the queen of the foreplay dissolve.

---

[20] 1. B, 2. A, 3. E (pre-Brad), 4. G (or maybe not), 5. C, 6. F, 7. D, 8. H

means. ✦ The terrifying power of the human sex drive is horrifically demonstra

If it weren't for pickpockets, I'd have no sex life at all.
—RODNEY DANGERFIELD

~•~

One day while Groucho Marx was working in his garden (dressed in well-worn gardening attire), a wealthy woman pulled up in a Cadillac and attempted to persuade the "gardener" to come and work for her. "How much does the lady of the house pay you?" she asked. "Oh, I don't get paid in dollars," Groucho replied, looking up. "She just lets me sleep with her."

~•~

It's the good girls who keep the diaries;
the bad girls never have the time.
—TALLULAH BANKHEAD

•••

True or False?

↪ *The Big Easy* was my first girlfriend's nickname.

↪ Fetus is a character on *Gunsmoke*.

↪ A condom is an apartment complex.

I know a man who gave up smoking, drinking, sex, and rich food. He was healthy right up to the day he killed himself.

—JOHNNY CARSON

~♦~

Bob Loblaw: Can you catalog for me the various ways you've been promised to be fulfilled whether or not said promise was made explicit?
Lindsay: You want me to be explicit?
Bob Loblaw: Yes, but I will be needing to get off in four minutes.
Lindsay: Well, let's see if I can hit that target for you.

—*ARRESTED DEVELOPMENT*

~♦~

Two's company. Three is fifty bucks.

—JOAN RIVERS

♦♦

Over the past few years, more money has been spent on breast implants and Viagra than is spent on Alzheimer's disease research; it is believed that by the year 2030 there will be a large number of people wandering around with huge breasts and erections—who can't remember what to do with them.

—ANDY ROONEY

be orgasmic. ♦ Why don't we both go somewhere where we can both be alone?

I'm at an age where food has taken the place of sex in my life.
In fact, I've just had a mirror put over my kitchen table.
—RODNEY DANGERFIELD

✦✦✦

I once made love for an hour and fifteen minutes, but it was
the night the clocks are set ahead.
—GARRY SHANDLING

✦✦

I'm at the age now where just putting my
cigar in its holder is a thrill.
—GEORGE BURNS

~✦~

*Q. How do you know when a male porn star is
at the gas station?*
*A. Right before the gas stops pumping, he pulls
out the nozzle and sprays it all over the car.*

~✦~

Could you shave or something? Every time
I blow you I feel like I'm flossing.
—*SEX AND THE CITY*

✦✦✦

I admire the hell out of the her. You can't have sex with
someone you admire.
—*SEINFELD*

Snarkin' the Facts

➢ *The average couple spends about twenty minutes engaged in sexual foreplay prior to intercourse. Does that include watching porn?*

➢ *When it comes to online porn, men are six times more likely than women to seek it out. And twelve times more likely to go blind.*

Sex is simple—love is painful.
—RON JEREMY

✦✦

Don't ask her if she came. You're a big boy now, Clouseau,
you should know if she came.
—DENNIS MILLER

~✦~

Q. *What have you got if you have two fuzzy
green balls in the palm of your hand?*
A. *Kermit's undivided attention.*

~✦~

Humans are the only animals who can
have sex over the phone.
—DAVID LETTERMAN

does not mean getting your wife drunk. ✦ Save your breath. . . . You'll need it

~•~

Heather: Hey, do you want to try it from behind?
Charlie: Absolutely. That's my favorite.
Heather: Me too.
Charlie: Right? Because it gets your spot, right?
Heather: Right, that yes, and because I can multitask. The e-mails just pile up if you don't get to them right away.

—CALIFORNICATION

~•~

It is said Paris Hilton doesn't pay for drinks when she goes out. Don't worry; she's still getting plenty of fluids.

—CONAN O'BRIEN

+++

I would have sex with sand before I have sex with Rosanne.

—HOWARD STERN

~•~

A woman goes to a doctor complaining about knee pains. "Do you indulge in any activities that puts pressure on your knees?" asks the doctor. "Well, my husband and I do it doggy style every night." "I see," said the doctor. "You know there are other sexual positions." "Not if you want to watch TV, there ain't."

~•~

w up your date. • My ex-boyfriend is the kind of a man that you would use as a

When authorities warn you of the sinfulness of sex,
there is an important lesson to be learned.
Do not have sex with the authorities.
—MATT GROENING

✦✦

Mae West

- ➢ I consider sex a misdemeanor; the more I miss, de meaner I get.

- ➢ To err is human—but it feels divine.

- ➢ I feel like a million tonight. But one at a time.

- ➢ An orgasm a day keeps the doctor away.

- ➢ I only like two kinds of men—domestic and imported.

- ➢ Thanks, I enjoyed every inch of it.

- ➢ I'm single because I was born that way.

- ➢ When it comes to men, she never turns down anything except the bedcovers.

- ➢ When women go wrong, men go right after them.

A girl's legs are her best friends, but even the
best of friends must part.
—REDD FOXX

✦✦✦

I have a tremendous sex drive. My boyfriend
lives forty miles away.
—PHYLLIS DILLER

✦✦

Hank: I do some of my best work from the bottom. You
know why? Hands free—it's like sexual Bluetooth.
—*CALIFORNICATION*

✦✦✦

It's been so long since I made love I can't
even remember who gets tied up.
—JOAN RIVERS

✦✦

Whenever women catfight, men think it's
going to turn to sex.
—YASMINE BLEETH

~✦~

*Jimmy Kimmel on Larry King's reconciliation
with Shawn King: "I don't know what brought
those two together, but I do know the makeup
sex was disgusting."*

~✦~

grand statement of his love for her. She was cold, hard, cracked, and only got

---

Things Not to Say During Sex

- ➤ So much for the fulfillment of sexual fantasies!

- ➤ I think you have it on backwards.

- ➤ When is this supposed to feel good?

- ➤ You're good enough to do this for a living!

- ➤ Is that blood on the headboard?

- ➤ Are you sure I don't know you from somewhere?

I'm dating a homeless woman. It's easier to
talk her into staying over.
—GARRY SHANDLING

~♦~

*At opposite ends of the earth, there are two
men: one is walking a tightrope between two
skyscrapers, and the other is getting a blow
job from an eighty-five-year-old woman. They
are each thinking the same thing—don't look
down!*

~♦~

plowed around the holidays. ♦ How can you tell if your husband's dead? Sex is t

~•~

Groucho Marx was having problems with premature ejaculation. Someone recommended a topical cream, guaranteed to prolong erection. When asked later if it worked, he replied, "I came rubbing the stuff on."

~•~

Joan Crawford has slept with every
male star at MGM except Lassie.
—BETTE DAVIS

♦♦♦

It isn't premarital sex if you have no intention
of getting married.
—GEORGE BURNS

♦♦

Sex COULD kill you. Do you know what the human body
goes through when you have sex? Pupils dilate, arteries
constrict, core temperature rises, heart races, blood pressure
skyrockets, respiration becomes rapid and shallow, the brain
fires bursts of electrical impulses from nowhere to nowhere,
and secretions spit out of every gland, and the muscles tense
and spasm like you're lifting three times your body weight.
It's violent. It's ugly. And it's messy. And if God hadn't made
it UNBELIEVABLY fun, the human race would have died
out eons ago.
—HOUSE

Snarkin' the News

↔ *MTV*, what hath thou wrought? They're casting for a spinoff of Jersey Shore that takes place in a nursing home with senior citizens. One scene: Fanny Goldblatt, eighty-nine, comes into the rec room with balled-up fists and says, "Whoever guesses what's in my hand can have sex with me." A disinterested Murray Fine says, "An elephant." Fanny says, "Close enough."

↔ A British magistrate was recently arrested with copious amounts of porn and video, all depicting women having sex with all manner of critter—dogs, horses, frogs (?), donkeys, and snakes. He was sentenced to a sex offender program and is currently remaking *Dr. Doolittle*, with the hit song "If I Can Talk Dirty to the Animals."

↔ Given the recent news of sex abuse scandal in the Boy Scouts, they are officially adopting "If you hear the sound of a zipper . . . be prepared" as their new motto.

WOMEN
ON
WOMEN

rpendicular expression of a horizontal desire. ⋅ The only difference between

WOMEN ON WOMEN

You can make the argument quite easily that there is no one snarkier than a woman discussing sex—especially when she's talking to another woman about women. You see, though the average heterosexual woman would be loath to admit to a man that she takes...a while...to climax...when she's talking about her inner oyster to another woman, the snarks can fly. Sisterhood, grrl power, feminist doctrine . . .when it comes to speaking frankly, women rule the roost. Take a look.

Now, many of you out there will claim that I added this chapter for myself. Not true. I added this chapter for all the men reading this.

It's so tiring to make love to women; it takes forever. I'm too lazy to be a lesbian.

—CAMILLE PAGLIA

Making love to a woman is like real estate— location, location, location.

—CAROL LEIFER

Some women can't say the word "lesbian"— even when their mouth is full of one.

—KATE CLINTON

---

the people I've dated and Charles Manson is that Manson has the decency to lo

Show me a woman who doesn't feel some guilt after sex, and I'll show you a man.

—ERICA JONG

Lead me not into temptation. I can find the way myself.

—RITA MAE BROWN

If male homosexuals are called "gay," then female homosexuals should be called "ecstatic."

—SHELLEY ROBERTS

It's a cosmic joke that I'm a lesbian, because I understand men so well but women are a complete mystery to me.

—LEA DELARIA

We are secretly glad Anne Heche is back on your team. She scares us.

She's not gay. She just ran out of men.

any woman can have: The older she gets, the more interested he is in her. • 5

Music and Performing Arts

> I always thought music was more important than sex—then
> I thought, if I don't hear a concert for a year and a half, it
> doesn't bother me.
> —JACKIE MASON

THIS CHAPTER FOCUSES ON a couple of muses—music and comedy—with both muses needing to be obeyed. I can hear it now . . . kind of a leap, Lar, no? No. Right off the bat, they are definitely not mutually exclusive, as much of today's music is a joke (ba-dum-bump . . . I'll be here all week).

So where does the sex come in? Well, sex has been THE subject of both music AND comedy since time immortal. The differences? Musicians get laid (a lot) and comedians . . . well comedians spend a lot of time not getting laid and being really pissed about it. It's enough to grab that mike stand between your legs and let the snark fly. Let's watch and listen.

Men don't realize that if we're sleeping with them
on the first date, we're probably not interested
in seeing them again either.
—CHELSEA HANDLER

+++

She got the gold mine, I got the shaft.
—JERRY REED

++

Love is not the dying moan of a distant violin—it's the
triumphant twang of a bedspring.
—S. J. PERELMAN

+++

I always knew Frank would end up in bed with a boy.
—AVA GARDNER ON SINATRA'S MARRIAGE
TO MIA FARROW

++

Disco provides a rhythmic accompaniment for the activities
of people who wish to gain access to each other for potential
future reproduction.
—FRANK ZAPPA

+++

Strippers should be role models for little girls. If only for the
fact that they wax their assholes.
—SARAH SILVERMAN

I'm not slutty at all. I've only slept with four men . . .
and that was a weird night.

—AMY SCHUMER

◆◆

You have between your legs the most
sensitive instrument known to man, and all
you can do is sit there and scratch it.

—SIR THOMAS BEECHAM TO A FEMALE CELLIST

~◆~

*A man and a woman are lying in bed after a
disappointing round of sex. "You've got a very
small organ," says the woman. The man replies,
"Yeah, well, I didn't know I'd be playing
Carnegie Hall."*

~◆~

There's nothing better than good sex . . . but bad sex? A
peanut-butter-and-jelly sandwich is better than bad sex.

—BILLY JOEL

◆◆◆

Losing my virginity was a career move.

—MADONNA

◆◆

I'd like to meet the man who invented sex and
see what he's working on now.

—GEORGE CARLIN

Five Songs Guaranteed to Kill the Mood

1. "Who Let the Dogs Out," Baha Men
2. "Thong Song," Sisqó
3. "Don't Worry, Be Happy," Bobby McFerrin
4. "Smack My Bitch Up," Prodigy
5. "We Are the World," USA for Africa

The best things in life are free . . . try explaining
that to an angry hooker.
—DANIEL BOKOR

✦✦✦

Women say they want a man who knows
what a woman's worth. That's a pimp.
—RICH HALL

✦✦

Don't leave a piece of jewelry at his house so you can go back
and get it later; he may be with his real girlfriend.
—AMY SEDARIS

✦✦✦

Oooh. Aaahhh. Get out.
—ANDREW DICE CLAY'S IMPRESSION OF
A ONE-NIGHT STAND

girls are bad girls that never get caught. ✦ There's a fine line between cuddling

My girlfriend can count all the lovers she's had on one hand—provided she's holding a calculator.
—TOM COTTER

++

Oysters are supposed to enhance sexual performance, but they don't work for me. Maybe I put them on too soon.
—GARRY SHANDLING

+++

I'm saving the bass player for Omaha.
—JANIS JOPLIN

++

You know more about a man in one night in bed than in months of conversation.
—EDITH PIAF

+++

I'm afraid of the video guy judging me because I don't want him to think I'm some sort of a freaky pervert. So now when I rent porn, I'll actually get *Dirty Debutantes* and *Citizen Kane*. He knows I'm a masturbating loser, but I'm a sophisticated masturbating loser.
—MARC MARON

Sexual Indiscretions Match Box[21]

A. Mackenzie Phillips   D. George Michael

B. Pamela Anderson   E. Kid Rock

C. Fred Durst   F. Rihanna

~•~

1. Limp Bizkit's front man sued when a repairman leaked his sex video. Not sure why—he could have proved once and for all that the name of his band wasn't based on his organ.

2. First, she was abused by her musician boyfriend, and then naked pictures appeared on the web. She defended them—and the boyfriend—by saying, "If you don't send your boyfriend naked pictures, then I feel bad for him." Ummm . . . okay.

3. Made not one but two sex tapes with rock stars of questionable talent if not endowment. Was then engaged to a third rock star. No report on his endowment.

4. Used both Oprah and a tell-all bio to reveal the news of a rape and subsequent decade-long affair with her pop star father.

5. A teen heartthrob that came out of the closet when he was caught and arrested for "lewd behavior" in the public toilet at a Beverly Hills park.

---

[21] 1. C, 2. F, 3. B, 4. A, 5. D, 6. E

6. A tape of him getting a blow job on his tour bus never got to DVD, but maybe that's because it contained "no sex" according to his now-former pal, Scott Stapp of Creed (who was also involved in the "nonsexual" action, along with four female groupies).

You know you gotta lose some weight when your
girlfriend wants to lick your titties.
—REGGIE MCFADDEN

♦♦

Oral sex should be an Olympic sport because it's harder than
curling, and if you're good at it, you deserve a medal.
—LEWIS BLACK

♦♦♦

My girlfriend was complaining about my stamina in the
sack, so I popped six Viagra and drank a six-pack of Red
Bull. Her funeral is Tuesday.
—HARLAN WILLIAMS

♦♦

Three minutes of serious sex and I need eight hours
of sleep and a giant bowl of Wheaties.
—RICHARD PRYOR

I tried phone sex—it gave me an ear infection.
—RICHARD LEWIS

+++

Told her the thing I loved most about her
was her mind . . . because that's what told her
to get into bed with me.
—STEVEN WRIGHT

++

I like my wine like my women—ready to pass out.
—ROBIN WILLIAMS

+++

I think we can all agree that sleeping around
is a great way to meet people.
—CHELSEA HANDLER

++

My boyfriend and I live together, which means we don't have
sex—ever. Now that the milk is free, we've both become
lactose intolerant.
—MARGARET CHO

~+~

Q: What did the bowlegged doe say?
A: That's the last time I do that for ten bucks.

~+~

I want to get an abortion. But my boyfriend and
I are having trouble conceiving.
—SARAH SILVERMAN

✦✦✦

Everybody loves you when they are about to come.
—MADONNA

✦✦

They're talking about banning cigarette smoking now in any
place that's used by ten or more people in a week, which, I
guess, means that Madonna can't even smoke in bed.
—BILL MAHER

✦✦✦

True or False?

↔ A G-string is part of a violin.

↔ Coitus is a musical instrument.

↔ Kotex is a radio station in Texas.

What is love but a second-hand emotion?
—TINA TURNER

dressing in front of men than they do undressing in front of other women. They

Snarkin' the News

↝ Ah yes, Courtney Love . . . I mean Courtney Michelle . . . said in an interview that homely girls are better at sex, that "us girls who grew up that way try harder. Pretty girls just lay there." I'm sure she has firsthand information . . . more people have gone down on her than on the *Titanic*.

↝ Lady Gaga said in an interview in *Vanity Fair* that she's refraining from sex because she worried that "if I sleep with someone, they're going to take my creativity away through my vagina." Off by inches, sweetie.

↝ George Michael has been arrested again in London for "possession of cannabis driving while unfit through drink or drugs." And guess what? It was in a bathroom! He should do a kids' book—*Everybody Poops . . . and Gets High.*

↝ Kevin Federline is expecting his fifth child—oops, I did it again . . . and again . . . and again . . .

Sex and drugs and rock and roll
Is all my brain and body need
Sex and drugs and rock and roll
Are very good indeed.
—IAN DURY

~♦~

Q: What is two-hundred-feet long and has no
pubic hair?
A: The front row at a Jonas Brothers concert.

~♦~

I don't know if it's the weather or what's going on—the
summer or something like that—but recently I've been
feeling extremely bisexual. I don't know what it is. I don't
know what's going on, but I walked down the street, and
suddenly, the ladies are looking awfully good to me.
—ANDY KINDLER

~♦~

His finest hour lasted a minute and a half.
—PHYLLIS DILLER

best thing on earth, but next to it. ♦ Impotence: Nature's way of saying "No

Chapters in Justin Bieber's New Book

Chapter 6—The Day My Face Broke Out
Chapter 10—My First Wet Dream
Chapter 12—Three Girls at Once
Chapter 14—The Day My Face Broke Out Again
Chapter 20—Learning to Drive
Chapter 21—Learning to Parallel Park
Chapter 22—Tipping My Driver
Chapter 30—Four Girls at Once
Chapter 35—The Day My Voice Changed and My Career
   Ended

It's okay to laugh in the bedroom as long
as you don't point.
—WILL DURST

++

The late porn star Johnny Wadd claimed to have been laid
fourteen thousand times. He died of friction.
—LARRY BROWN

+++

I'm not kinky, but occasionally I like to put on a robe and
stand in front of a tennis ball machine.
—GARRY SHANDLING

hard feelings." • Two years ago I married a lovely young virgin, and if that does

I go from stool to stool in singles bars, trying to get lucky, but there's never any gum under any of them.
—EMO PHILIPS

··

I'm fed up with men that use sex as a sleeping pill.
—TONI BRAXTON

···

There we were in the middle of a sexual revolution wearing clothes that guaranteed we wouldn't get laid.
—DENIS LEARY

··

Masturbation is always safe. You not only control the person you're with, but you can also leave when you want to.
—DUDLEY MOORE

···

The closest I ever came to a menage-a-trois was when I dated a schizophrenic.
—RITA RUDNER

··

I was like, Am I gay? Am I straight? And I realized...I'm just slutty. Where's my parade?
—MARGARET CHO

"I think I'd rather get run over by a train."
—MADONNA, ON WHETHER SHE
PLANS TO MARRY AGAIN

✦✦✦

It's weird when you watch women's tennis now, with all the grunting and shouting. It's like phone sex. You have to be very careful not to get too excited.
—ROBIN WILLIAMS

✦✦

A lot of people say, 'I would rather have a heart attack at the height of sexual passion'. I think I would prefer to be killed by a bookcase.
—TOM STOPPARD, ON THE IDEAL WAY TO DIE.

her speechless. ✦ I hope I'm the last guy on earth -- I wanna see if all those

MEN ON MEN

Unlike women who can stay completely open to all the possibilities that might be found in a sexual adventure within their own gender, most men tend to shy away from these trysts. Sometimes vehemently. On top of which, men would rather have a root canal than discuss their own sex life.

While most men love to have sex and many even love to watch it . . . the last thing men want to do is talk about it. At least in any way that isn't bragging, boasting, or macho posturing. Feelings? Emotions? Nah. Leave that to the fairer sex . . . and how about them Bears?

It is impossible to obtain a conviction for sodomy from an English jury. Half of them don't believe that it can physically be done, and the other half is doing it.

—WINSTON CHURCHILL

I'm glad I'm not bisexual— I couldn't stand being rejected by men as well as women.

—BERNARD MANNING

If you have sex with your clone, are you gay or are you masturbating?

Why is it so hard for women to find men who are sensitive and caring? Because those men already have boyfriends.

Spaghetti is straight too— until you heat it up.

My cousin is an agoraphobic homosexual, which makes it kind of hard for him to come out of the closet.

—BILL KELLY

The guy runs a prison. He can have any piece of ass he wants.

—ARRESTED DEVELOPMENT

It's just a penis, right? Probably no worse for you than smoking.

—DAVID SEDARIS

nt to go home and those who don't. The trouble is, they are usually married to

each other. ✦ You have two choices in life: You can stay single and be miserable,

Politics and Religion

How did sex come to be thought of as dirty in the first
place? God must have been a Republican.
—WILL DURST

THE CLICHÉS RUN RAMPANT. "He's a candidate for the people." "He'll bring dignity to the office." "He's a man of great moral fiber." Right. Politics have always made for strange bedfellows . . . and most of the problems seem to start in and around the bed . . . or beds . . . or public men's rooms. Once caught, they all seem to fall back on this one forgiving saw: "As the Bible says, 'Let he who is without sin cast the first stone.'"

Which brings us nicely into the cohort of this chapter—religion. Night and day? Or holy water with ice cubes and a splash of bourbon? You be the judge.

Clinton lied. A man might forget where he parks or where he lives, but he never forgets oral sex, no matter how bad it is.

—BARBARA BUSH[22]

+++

I'm like President Ford: I can't do two things at once. I can't have intercourse and enjoy myself at the same time.

—RICHARD LEWIS

++

Sex is a bad thing because it rumples the clothes.

—JACQUELINE KENNEDY ONASSIS

~+~

On election eve, 1948, Thomas Dewey (who, according to polls, was poised to defeat Harry Truman for the presidency) turned to his wife and asked, "How will it be to sleep with the President of the United States?" "A high honor," she replied, "and quite frankly, darling, I'm looking forward to it." On the following morning, after the news arrived of the election results and Truman had won, they sat down for breakfast. Mrs. Dewey said with a smile, "Tell me, Tom, am I going to Washington, or is Harry coming here?"

~+~

---

[22]   My, oh my, Babs!

over experience. ◆ Sex is like software: For every one who pays for it there

Things Not to Say During Sex

➢ Does this count as a date?

➢ Have you seen *Fatal Attraction*?

➢ Sorry about the tags, I'm not very good with names.

➢ Don't mind me . . . I always file my nails in bed.

➢ I hope I didn't forget to turn the gas oven off. Do you have a light?

➢ You could at least *act* like you're enjoying it!

When women get depressed, they either shop or eat.
Men invade another country.
—ELAYNE BOOSLER

✦✦✦

When you're away, I'm restless, lonely,
Wretched, bored, dejected; only
Here's the rub, my darling dear,
I feel the same when you are here.
—SAMUEL HOFFENSTEIN

The art of making love, muffled up in furs, in the open air, with the thermometer at zero, is a Yankee invention.
—JOHN QUINCY ADAMS

♦♦

Some of us are becoming the men we wanted to marry.
—GLORIA STEINEM

♦♦♦

As one gets older, litigation replaces sex.
—GORE VIDAL

~♦~

Two nuns ride their bikes down a lane. The first nun says, "I've never come this way before!" The second nun says, "Oh, it must be the cobblestone."

~♦~

I thank God I was raised Catholic, so sex will always be dirty.
—JOHN WATERS

♦♦

Sex is not some sort of pristine, reverent ritual. You want reverent and pristine, go to church.
—CYNTHIA HEIMEL

My girlfriend asked me, "Do You believe in love at first sight"? I said, "At the f

~✦~

President Calvin Coolidge and his wife visited a government farm one day and were taken around on separate tours. Mrs. Coolidge, passing the chicken pens, inquired of the keeper whether the roosters copulated more than once a day. "Yes," the man said. "Dozens of times." "Tell that," Mrs. Coolidge replied, "to the president!" Sometime later, the president, passing the same pens, was told about the roosters—and about his wife's remark. "Same hen every time?" he asked. "Oh no, a different one each time," the keeper replied. "Tell that," Coolidge said with a sly nod, "to Mrs. Coolidge."

~✦~

God created sex. Priests created marriage.
—VOLTAIRE

✦✦✦

Grown men should not be having sex with prostitutes unless they are married to them.
—JERRY FALWELL

✦✦

I think God is a callous bitch for not making me a lesbian. I'm deeply disappointed by my sexual interest in men.
—DIAMANDA GALAS

Snarkin' the Facts

> ➤ According to the books, in Fairbanks, Alaska, it's illegal for moose to have sex on the city sidewalks. Let 'em get a hotel room like everyone else.

> ➤ One report states that 48 percent of women have faked an orgasm at least once in their life. Interestingly, an identical 48 percent of men also report faking an orgasm at least once. How funny would it be if all 48 percent were faking it together?

> ➤ On average, adult men think about sex every seven seconds. The figure is higher for politicians. There. And again. And again. Once more. And again. And . . . ahhhhh. And again. And again . . .

> ➤ A British study says that more than 25% of strippers there have a college degree. Many say it helps them earn more money because "80% of the guys just want to talk." Right...nothing relieves a hard-on faster than a conversation about our political system or the meaning of life.

Sometimes when I look at all my children I say to myself,
"Lillian, you should have stayed a virgin."
—LILLIAN CARTER[23]

+++

To hear religious people talk, one would think
God created the torso, head, legs, and arms;
but the devil slapped on the genitals.
—DON SCHRADER

++

Give me chastity and continence—but not yet.
—SAINT AUGUSTINE

+++

Christ died for our sins. Dare we make his martyrdom
meaningless by not committing them?
—JULES FEIFFER

++

Jesse Helms and Newt Gingrich were shaking hands,
congratulating themselves on the introduction of an antigay
bill in Congress. If it passes, they won't be able to shake
hands: it'll be illegal for a prick to touch an asshole.
—JUDY CARTER

---

[23] Jimmy had to be thinking "what's worse? Shit my brother does or
shit my mother says?")

ng around the finger does not cause a nerve block to the genitals. • Love your

Who Said What?[24]

A. George H. W. Bush	F. Gary Hart
B. Arnold Schwarzenegger	G. Sarah Palin
C. Marilyn Quayle	H. John Kennedy
D. Ted Kennedy	I. George W. Bush
E. Jimmy Carter	J. President Bill Clinton

~•~

1. If I don't have a woman every three days or so, I get a terrible headache.
2. They don't call me Tyrannosaurus Sex for nothing.
3. Too many good docs are getting out of the business. Too many ob-gyn aren't able to practice their love with women all across this country.
4. He would rather play golf than have sex any day.
5. Well, there was no sex for fourteen days.
6. This attractive lady whom I had only recently been introduced to dropped into my lap . . . I chose not to dump her off.

---

[24] 1. H; 2. D; 3. I; 4. C, on Vice President Dan Quayle; 5. B, on getting the cold shoulder from his wife after backing President George W. Bush at the Republican Convention; 6. F, referring to an encounter with Donna Rice; 7. A; 8. E; 9. J, during his 1998 grand jury testimony on the Monica Lewinsky affair 10. G

7. For seven and a half years I've worked alongside President Reagan. We've had triumphs. Made some mistakes. We've had some sex . . . uh . . . setbacks.

8. I've looked on many women with lust. I've committed adultery in my heart many times. God knows I will do this and forgives me.

9. It depends on what the meaning of the word "is" is.

10. The explicit sex-ed programs will not find my support.

~+~

The male lion can have sex as often as 100 times a day. In fact, at 103 times a day, the other animals stop calling him "King of the Jungle" and start calling him "President of the United States."

~+~

Sex: the pleasure is momentary, the position ridiculous, and the expense damnable.
—LORD CHESTERFIELD

+++

The only woman worth seeing undressed is the one you have undressed yourself.
—THE DUCHESS OF WINDSOR

Snarkin' the News

↪ Officials in a Texas town ordered the owners of a lingerie shop to get a food permit for edible undies they've been selling. Are they still around and do people still buy them? I seem to remember some comic who had a line that "even during sex, Americans can't stop eating." Plus, it's hard to get that stuff out of your beard.

↪ Indiana congressman Mark Souder resigned after having an affair with one of his aides, although he claims he didn't lie. When asked about her originally, he responded, "She's on my staff."

↪ Indonesian officials have stated that you can't join the army or become a police officer if you've had a penis enlargement. This is their new "one baton to a man" law that just went into effect. In weirdly related news, a Scottish man was arrested for weighing his Johnson on a grocery store produce scale. His sentence? He begins basic training in the Indonesian army next week.

↪ Police were called to a park in Washington after reports that a naked woman was tied to a tree while a man bit her. No one was arrested as it was determined "consensual"—perhaps the bark wasn't as bad as his bite.

Man—a creature made at the end of the week's work
when God was tired.
—MARK TWAIN

◆◆

God created man—but I can do better.
—ERMA BOMBECK

~◆~

*A hotline has been set up in Paris where you
can call and confess your sins immediately
after you get off a sex chat line. The number is
1-800-FORGIVE. Be careful, though—1-900-
FORGIVE is an entirely different call.*

~◆~

There will be sex after death; we just won't be able to feel it.
—LILY TOMLIN

The Bible contains six admonishments to homosexuals and 362 admonishments to heterosexuals. That doesn't mean that God doesn't love heterosexuals. It's just that they need more supervision.

—LYNN LAVNER

✦✦✦

You know why God is a man? Because if God was a woman, she would have made sperm taste like chocolate.

—CARRIE SNOW

✦✦

True or False?

↪ Semen is another word for "sailor."

↪ A menstrual cycle has three wheels.

↪ An umbilical cord is part of a parachute.

No matter how much catfights, there always seem to be plenty of kittens.

—ABRAHAM LINCOLN

best when she is at her worst. ✦ We have orgasms because how else would we kn

Why was man created on the last day? So that he can be told, when pride possesses him, God created the gnat before thee.

—THE TALMUD[25]

~+~

Several years ago, Reagan, Bush, and Clinton all went on a cruise together. While the ship was out in the sea, it hit an iceberg and started to sink. Quickly, Reagan yelled out, "Women and children first!" Bush then cried, "Screw the women!" To which, Clinton responded, "Do you think we have time?"

~+~

Do television evangelists do more than lay people?

—STANLEY RALPH ROSS

++

Philosophy is to the real world as masturbation is to sex.

—KARL MARX

+++

He that falls in love with himself will have no rivals.

—BENJAMIN FRANKLIN

---

[25] Yikes, snark from above!

When asked if they would like to have sex with me, 30% of women said, 'Yes', while the other 70% replied, 'Again?'
—SILVIO BERLUSCONI

++

I've learned a lot about women. I think I've learned exactly how the fall of man occurred in the Garden of Eden. Adam and Eve were in the Garden of Eden, and Adam said one day, "Wow, Eve, here we are, at one with nature, at one with God. We'll never age, we'll never die, and all our dreams come true the instant that we have them." And Eve said, "Yeah . . . it's just not enough, is it?"
—BILL HICKS

+++

Snarkin' the News

↪ A church group, called Victory over Porn Addiction, has come under fire as a possible money-making con scheme. The Kansas DA has started to look into its validity. "There are a lot of these groups out there. You rub one out and a little while later you're at it again."

↪ A sex shop in Amsterdam held a promotion where they gave away two thousand "pope condoms," perfect for playing Hide the Bishop.

wine, women, and song; mostly song. ♦ If the effort that went in research on t

↔ An Iranian cleric says that women who dress in provocative clothing are promiscuous, encourage premarital sex and adultery and are the reasons they have been experiencing multiple earthquakes. Well, thankfully someone has finally cleared up the whole California thing.

↔ Newt Gingrich now says his passion for the country contributed to his marital infidelity. Huh? "So, my fellow Americans, if elected president as an uber-patriotic American, I'll be screwing just about everybody, all in the name of passionate patriotism." "My country tis of thee, I love adultery, It makes me hard." The eleventh commandment: "Thou shalt not admit adultery."

↔ A group in San Francisco has succeeded in getting a proposal on the fall ballot that would ban circumcision. If passed, anyone caught performing one would be fined $1,000—plus tip.

↔ Eric Massa resigned recently, and his male co-workers are just tickled pink about it. Word was he was quite hard on the members of his staff.

male bosom had gone into our space program, we would now be running hotdog

I'm going to Iowa for an award. Then I'm appearing
at Carnegie Hall, it's sold out. Then I'm sailing to France
to be honored by the French government. I'd give it all
up for one erection.
—GROUCHO MARX

++

Male misconceptions

➢ Roe vs. Wade is NOT two ways to cross a river.

➢ "Harass" is NOT two words.

➢ Safe sex does NOT mean a padded headboard.

➢ Foreplay is NOT a half hour of begging.

ow. • Wedding Cake: food that diminishes a woman's sex drive by 90%. • Love

MEN ON WOMEN

The battle of the sexes rages on. And boy, is everyone pissed or what? Men always think they get the short end of the stick. (Maybe I should rephrase?) How about . . . men always feel they get the shaft. (Nope, not working.)

Anyway, if you're not getting any, your snark meter will be turned up to 11. These are a few of my favorite snarks . . . from the male point of view.

A man is as old as the women he feels.

—GROUCHO MARX

Men have more problems than women. In the first place, they have to put up with women.

—FRANCOISE SAGAN

A DYSLEXIC MAN WALKS INTO A BRA . . .

I have no luck with women. I once went on a date and asked the woman if she'd brought any protection. She pulled a switchblade on me.

—SCOTT ROEBEN

comes in spurts. ♦ Never argue with a woman when she's tired . . . or rested. ♦

Every so often, I try to masturbate a large word into conversation, even if I'm not really sure what it means.

+

Spouse: someone who'll stand by you through all the trouble you wouldn't have had if you'd stayed single.

To me, a woman's body is a temple. I try to attend services as often as I can.

—WILL SHRINER

+

I think sex is better than logic, but I can't prove it.

+

Woman was God's second mistake.

—NEITZSCHE

How do you know if it's time to wash the dishes and clean your house? Look inside your pants. If there's a penis there, it's not time.

Whatmendesireisavirgin who is a whore.

Love is very deep, but sex only has to go a few inches.

alities that most attract a woman to a man are usually the same ones she can't

No matter how good she looks, some other guy is sick and tired of putting up with her shit.

✦

Men say of women what pleases them; women do with men what pleases them.

✦

There's one consolation about matrimony. When you look around you can always see somebody who did worse.

—WARREN H. GOLDSMITH

Ah, women. They make the highs higher and the lows more frequent.

—FRIEDRICH NIETZSCHE

✦

I'm all for bringing back the birch, but only between consenting adults.

—GORE VIDAL

✦

When making love, most married men fantasize that their wives aren't fantasizing.

Love: the sickest of Irony's sick jokes. The place where logic and order go to die.

—CHRISTOPHER MOORE

Some don't prefer the pursuit of happiness to the happiness of pursuit.

THE MOST HAPPY MARRIAGE I CAN PICTURE OR IMAGINE TO MYSELF WOULD BE THE UNION OF A DEAF MAN TO A BLIND WOMAN.

—SAMUEL TAYLOR COLERIDGE

I'm always looking for meaningful one night stands.

—DUDLEY MOORE

Falling in love is so hard on the knees.

—AEROSMITH

ood. ◆ Everyone in favor of birth control has already been born. ◆ I know how

to satisfy my wife in bed. I leave. ♦ My wife put a mirror over our bed . . . she lik

Sports and Miscellany

The trouble is not that players have sex the night before a game. It's that they stay out all night looking for it.

—CASEY STENGEL

SOME OF YOU OUT there might say that sex and sports are incongruous.[26] And some of you might ask me what "incongruous" means. But I think that not only do sports and sex go together, but that someone should start a movement to get sex added to the Olympics. Ski in tandem a mile, jump each other's bones, ski another mile. First to finish gets the medal. All tens.

You'll find some other funny stuff here that didn't really fit in other chapters. Deal with it. I have.

---

[26] If that's the case, consider this chapter miscellany. Because sex is nothing if not miscellaneous.

I like my sex the way I play basketball, one on one
with as little dribbling as possible.
—LESLIE NIELSEN

♦♦♦

Match the Sex Euphemism to the Sport[27]

A. Soccer	E. Baseball
B. Most sports	F. Basketball
C. Football	G. Golf
D. Boxing	H. Hockey

~♦~

1. Pitcher or catcher?
2. Putting from the rough.
3. Pulling the goalie.
4. Take one for the team.
5. Take it to the hole.
6. Stuffed it in the end zone.
7. Deep in the hole.
8. Hitting the canvas.

---

[27] 1. E, 2. G, 3. H, 4. B, 5. F, 6. C, 7. A, 8. D

Amish woman's fantasy? Two Mennonite. ♦ The definition of wicker box? Wh.

Hitting is better than sex.
—REGGIE JACKSON

++

The point of using the number was to show that sex was a
great part of my life as basketball was a great part of my life.
That's the reason why I was single.
—WILT CHAMBERLAIN[28]

~+~

*According to Runner's World magazine, two
out of three runners say that they fantasize
about sex while running. On the other hand,
only one out of eleven fantasizes about running
while having sex.(And nine out of ten fantasize
about sex while running a bath)*

~+~

Fifty percent of life in the NBA is sex.
The other 50 percent is money.
—DENNIS RODMAN

+++

My boyfriend is so into fantasy football; he makes noises
while playing it that he doesn't even make during sex.
—GIULIA ROZZI

---

[28] 20,000 women? When did he have time for basketball?

mer Fudd wants to do to Petunia Pig. • If love is the answer, can you rephrase

Sports Clichés That Could Be About Sex

> Practice as if you are the worst; perform as if you are the best.
> —JOHN WOODEN

✦✦

> It is deceptively simple and endlessly complicated; it satisfies the soul and frustrates the intellect. It is at the same time rewarding and maddening—and it is, without a doubt, the greatest game mankind has ever invented.
> —ARNOLD PALMER

✦✦✦

> It has nothing to do with fair play. It is bound up with hatred, jealousy, boastfulness, disregard of all rules, and sadistic pleasure in witnessing violence. In other words, it is war minus the shooting.
> —GEORGE ORWELL

✦✦

> If you aren't playing well, it isn't as much fun. When that happens, I tell myself just to go out and play as I did when I was a kid.
> —THOMAS WATSON

✦✦✦

➤ We didn't lose the game; we just ran out of time.
—VINCE LOMBARDI

✦✦

➤ If everything seems under control, you're just not going fast enough.
—MARIO ANDRETTI

✦✦✦

➤ If you're not just a little bit nervous before a match, you probably don't have the expectations of yourself that you should have.
—HALE IRWIN

✦✦✦

➤ Adversity causes some men to break; others to break records.
—WILLIAM A. WARD

✦✦

➤ Nobody's a natural. You work hard to get good and then work to get better. It's hard to stay on top.
—PAUL COFFEY

✦✦✦

➤ The biggest things are often the easiest to do because there is so little competition.
—WILLIAM VAN HORNE

✦✦

➢ It breaks your heart. It is designed to break your heart. The game begins in the spring when everything else begins again, and it blossoms in the summer, filling the afternoons and evenings, and then as soon as the chill rains come, it stops and leaves you to face the fall alone.

—A. BARTLETT GIAMATTI

✦✦✦

➢ Quick guys get tired; big guys don't shrink.

—MARV HARSHMAN

~✦~

Q. How do you find a blind man in a nudist colony?
A. It's not hard.

~✦~

The reason guys like women in leather outfits so much is because they have that new-car smell.

—GEORGE FARA

✦✦✦

We were having sex doggie style. I didn't plan on it; it's just how she passed out.

—DAVE ATTEL

✦✦

chopsticks; it looks easy until you try it. • Don't make love by the garden gate, lo

Match the Punchline to the Joke[29]

A. Fast pucks   D. Ten minutes of silence
B. Snowballs   E. Tulips on your organ
C. Your Grip   F. Yankee

~•~

1. What's better than a rose on your piano?
2. What's the best thing about a blow job?
3. What's the same thing as a quickie but a guy can do it himself?
4. What's the difference between a female snowman and a male snowman?
5. What is the difference between a hockey game and a high school reunion?
6. What's the difference between pink and purple?

The amazing thing is, when you learn to masturbate in a shower, it only takes a minute before the rest of the team is kicking your ass.

—RAY JAMES

••

[29]   1. E, 2. D, 3. F, 4. B, 5. A, 6. C

blind but the neighbors ain't.   • I love you no matter what you do but do you have

The golf swing is like sex. You can't be thinking
about the mechanics of the act while you
are performing.
—DAVE HILL

✦✦✦

Snarkin' the Facts

> ➢ It takes a sperm one hour to swim seven inches. More
> if it involves the backstroke.

> ➢ Americans spend twice as much money on pornogra-
> phy than they do on cookies. (It takes almost the same
> amount of time to clean the bed up after both.)

> ➢ The average size of an erect penis measures between 5
> and 6 inches, while the average size of a flaccid penis
> is about 3.5 inches. Unless, of course, you use a tape
> measure . . . then they're all 8 inches plus.

> ➢ The average male produces several million new sperm
> daily. Man, it's amazing the penis doesn't just burst.

> ➢ Statistics show that approximately 90 percent of men
> and 65 percent of women masturbate from time to
> time. I believe that stat for women. For men, "time to
> time" means first thing in the morning to the last thing
> at night.

> According to Kinsey, only 10 percent of the population is exclusively hetero- or homosexual. Makes sense—most people can't even decide what to order at the diner.

> Americans spend twice as much money on pornography than they do on cookies. It takes almost the same amount of time to clean the bed up after both.

> Masters and Johnson's stages of the sexual response cycle are excitement, plateau, orgasm, and resolution. Hey, let's not forget begging, pleading, crying, and apologizing.

> Ingredients in chocolate are proven to cause arousal similar in effect to sexual foreplay. In fact, some experts believe chocolate may be even more effective than foreplay for sexual arousal. Study conducted by the Hershey Corp. and Godiva.

A surgeon of some imprecision
Decided on self-circumcision.
A slip of the knife—
"Oh, dear," said his wife,
"Our sex life will need some revision."

✦✦✦

Usually I'm on top to keep the guy from escaping.
—LISA LAMPANELLI

✦✦

True or False?

↔ "Spread eagle" is an extinct bird.

↔ Testicles are found on an octopus.

↔ A clitoris is a type of flower.

Have you ever dated someone because you
were too lazy to commit suicide?
—JUDY TENUTA

✦✦

Oral sex is a great way to tone up your cheekbones.
—CYNTHIA HEIMEL

✦✦✦

I'm a married man. ✦ Hell hath no fury like the lawyer of a woman scorned. ✦ Tir

Snarkin' the News

↔ Paris Hilton is launching a new shoe line. These are the first shoes designed to look good when placed behind a woman's ears.

↔ A shipment of Viagra was hijacked last week. The police are looking for two hardened criminals.

↔ A sex shop in Alabama has come up with a novel way of selling its sex toys—through a drive-up window. Patrons can order from a menu of toys, lubricants, and stimulants. Whatever you do, do not ask for your order to be super sized. Ouch.

↔ Golfer John Daly's ex-wife has written a tell-all book about his degenerate exploits: passing out drunk at charity events, urinating on courses, taking strippers and escorts to exclusive country clubs—jeez, who does he think he is, Alice Cooper?

↔ A British man has opened a hotel for chickens, citing the fact that more and more people are now keeping them as pets and need a place for them when they travel. He charges an overnight fee but also has a four-hour rate . . . you know, for when there's eggs that just want to get laid.

~✦~

A bus stops and two Italian men get on. They seat themselves and engage in animated conversation. The lady sitting behind them ignores their conversation at first, but the she hears one of the men say the following: "Emma comes first. Denna I come. Two asses, they come together. I come again. Two asses, they come together again. I come again and pee twice. Then I come once a-more."

"You foulmouthed swine," retorted the lady indignantly. "In this country, we don't talk about our sex lives in public!"

"Hey, coola down, lady," said the man.

"Imma justa tellun my friend howa to spella 'Mississippi.'"

~✦~

Some condoms are made of sheep intestines,
but I was so scared the first time, I wore the whole sheep.
—DANNY WILLIAMS

✦✦✦

Play with each other. Play with yourselves. Just don't play
with the squirrels, they bite.

✦✦

down menus and on-line help. ✦ Women typically like the simple things in lif

Masturbation is like procrastination; it's all good and fun
until you realize you are only fucking yourself.

✦✦✦

Love at first sight may be possible, but I
feel a lot stronger about lust at first sight.
—XAVIERA HOLLANDER

~✦~

*"Do you have any batteries?" a woman asked
the hardware store clerk.*

*"Yes." The clerk gestures with his finger.
"Can you come this way?"*

*"If I could come that way," the woman
says, "I wouldn't need the batteries."*

~✦~

Mr. Right is now a guy who hasn't been laid in fifteen years.
—ELAYNE BOOSLER

✦✦

My classmates would copulate with anything that moved,
but I never saw any reason to limit myself.
—EMO PHILLIPS

~✦~

*Q. Three words to ruin a man's ego . . .
A. "Is it in?"*

~•~

Anyone who says that gratuitous sex is no substitute
for gratuitous violence obviously hasn't had enough
gratuitous sex.

—GEOFF SPEAR

•••

In sex as in banking, there is a penalty for early withdrawal.

—CYNTHIA NELMS

~•~

*There's a student in medical school who wants
to specialize in sexual disorders, so he makes
arrangements to visit the sexual disorder clinic.*

*The chief doctor is showing him around,
discussing cases and the facility, when the
student sees a patient masturbating right there
in the hallway.*

*"What condition does he have?" the
student asks.*

*"He suffers from seminal buildup disorder,"
the doctor replies. "If he doesn't obtain sexual
release forty to fifty times a day, he'll pass into
a coma."*

*The student takes some notes on that, and
they continue down the hall. As they turn the*

corner, he sees another patient with his pants around his ankles, receiving oral sex from a beautiful nurse.

"What about him?" the student asks. "What's his story?"

"Oh, it's the same condition," the doctor replies. "He just has a better health plan."

~•~

What's the most popular pastime in America?
Autoeroticism, hands down.
—SCOTT ROEBEN

~•~

Q: What's the difference between a tire and 365 used condoms?
A: One's a Goodyear and the other is a fucking great year!

~•~

I'm dating a woman now who, evidently, is unaware of it.
—GARRY SHANDLING

••

Forget love, I'd rather fall in chocolate.
—SANDRA J. DYKES

•••

The reason people sweat is so they won't catch
fire when making love.
—DON ROSE

✦✦✦

It's silly to have a mirror over your bed . . .
what are you going to do, shave?
—BILL COSBY

~✦~

*A seventy-five-year-old man went to his favorite
bar and met a woman with whom he hit if off
real well. They went to her place and had sex.
The old man tried and tried, but he could not
achieve orgasm. A few days later, he noticed a
drip at the end of his penis, so he went to see
the doctor about this oddity. The doctor asked
him if he had sex recently, and the old man said
that he had.*

*"Do you remember who the woman was
and where she lived?" the doctor asked.*

"Sure do," replied the old man.

*"Then you better get over there right away,"
said the doctor. "You're about to come."*

~✦~

I was actually dating a porn star for a while but here's the
problem . . . Y'know when most girls come home from a
hard day at work their feet are hurting? So I'm single.
—RUSSELL PETERS

✦✦

---

anxiety, n.: The first time you can't do it a second time.
panic, n.: The second time you can't do it the first time.

True or False?

↦ Douche is the Italian word for "twelve."

↦ Genitals are people of non-Jewish origins.

↦ Pubic hair is a wild rabbit.

In reality, everyone is good in bed. Close eyes. Shutdown
brain. Pause as necessary. Restart brain. Open eyes. What is
there to not be good at? Bed is the one place where laziness
is rewarded.
—JOHN DOBBIN

revent sin. It only prevents you from enjoying it. ✦ Kids in the back seat cause

~♦~

Q: *What's the difference between a bar and a clitoris?*

A: *Most men have no trouble finding a bar.*

~♦~

Where should one use perfume?
Wherever one wants to be kissed.
—COCO CHANEL

♦♦♦

Using Viagra is like putting a new flagpole on a condemned building.
—HARVEY KORMAN

~♦~

Two elderly men were talking about Viagra. One had never heard of it and asked the other what it was for.

"It's the greatest invention ever. It makes you feel like a man of thirty."

"Can you get it over the counter?"

"Probably—if you took two."

~♦~

Of course, men name their penis. Would you want to be bossed around by someone you don't know?
—MAGGIE PALEY

Snarkin' the News

↝ Scientists in Europe are working on a way to test for STDs through your cell. Besides what I imagine would be really an uncomfortable process, do you really want to have a gonorrhea app on your phone?

↝ A Dutch study has recently found that "gaydar," the ability to innately recognize sexual orientation, does, in fact, exist. However, in an effort to stay current, it will now be referred to as "gay-GPS."

↝ A woman was pulled over and arrested for trying to shave her "down there" area while driving to meet her boyfriend in Key West. She's lucky she didn't end up with the Bermuda Triangle.

Before sleeping together, people should boil themselves.
—RICHARD LEWIS

♦♦

Shopping is better than sex. At least if you're not satisfied, you can exchange it for something you really like.
—ADRIENNE GUSOFF

♦♦♦

ard to please - She replied, " I don't know. I've never tried." ♦ Darling, I can please

~•~

A woman goes to a doctor. "Doctor, every time I sneeze, I have an orgasm." The doctor is intrigued. "What are you taking for it?" he asks. The woman replies, "Pepper."

~•~

While Titian was grinding rose madder
His model was posed on a ladder
Her position to Titian
Suggested coition
So he dashed up the ladder and had her.

Q. *What gets longer when pulled, fits between a woman's breasts, inserts neatly in a hole and works best when jerked hard?*
A. *A seatbelt.*

~•~

The species of whale known as the black right whale has four kilos of brains and 1,000 kilos of testicles. If it thinks at all, we know what it is thinking about.

—JON LIEN

Euphemisms for Losing Your Virginity

➢ Throwing out the first pitch

➢ Moving out of Palmdale

➢ Learning to work the childproof containers

➢ Serving cherry delight

➢ Presenting Mr. Happy the key to the Furry City

➢ Finally having your weapon inspected

➢ Removing the training wheels from the pie cycle

➢ Taking the NasTea plunge

➢ Getting the VIP tour at Neverland

➢ Attending the Bush Inaugural Ball

➢ Fornication for $1,000, Alex

➢ Landing the Martian probe on Venus

cher. ✦ If a man, alone in the woods, says something and there isn't a woman

News flash: A man just flashed three women who were sitting on a bench. Two had a stroke but the other couldn't reach.

~+~

She's more interested in spice than spouse.

++

He's handsome. When she wants money, he has to hand some over.

+++

Their marriage is a partnership—he's the silent partner.

++

He should have known she was jealous—she had male bridesmaids.

+++

His towels are monogrammed—His, Hers, and Next.

++

He's the salt of the earth—she's been trying to shake him forever.

+++

Terminal bachelor—footloose and fiancé free.

++

Always look before you lip.

**SEX
BEFORE
LOVE**

eful comes out of it, but that's not the reason we're doing it. • Married men

SEX BEFORE LOVE

Remember that childhood ditty I mentioned earlier? "First comes *love*, then comes *marriage* . . ?" Is it really a simple song from the playground or a life sentence? Either way, it's wrong. First comes sex. Stop there. Used to be—for women, or so everyone thought—that love and sex were inseparable. Couldn't have one without the other. Went together like bread and butter, sugar and spice, Martin and Lewis (?) . . . well, you know, stuff that goes together. In order to indulge in that one most intimate thing between two people, there needed to be love . . . (sigh). Well, new day, new rules. Women of today are the same as men of forever . . . sex and love don't always have to be in the same room and still everybody still wins. Men have always only needed a time and a place. Anytime and anyplace. Women, welcome to the club. It's a pleasure to have you.

Sex is the most beautiful thing that can take place between a happily married man and his secretary.

– BARRY HUMPHRIES

A man can sleep around, no questions asked, but if a woman makes nineteen or twenty mistakes she's a tramp.

—CAROL SUSSKIND

Love is a matter of chemistry, but sex is a matter of physics.

"You're what?!?" is the most common form of marriage proposal.

BED IS THE POOR MAN'S OPERA.

should forget all their mistakes . . . there's no use in having two people who nev

Sex is like food: when you abstain, even the worst begins to look good.

The last thing I want to do is hurt you. But it's still on the list.

Will have sex for self-esteem.

Be naughty, save Santa a trip.

Sex on the whole was meant to be short, nasty and brutish. If what you want is cuddling . . . buy a puppy.

—JULIE BURCHILL

A woman occasionally is quite a serviceable substitute for masturbation.

Sex is like math: you add the bed, subtract the clothes, divide the legs and pray you don't multiply!

—FERAS YAGHMOUR

MATRIMONIAL-HARMONICS.

bra size and intelligence? The larger the bra she wears, the dumber the guy sh

Divorce

Divorce is a sacred institution between a man
and a woman who hate each other.
—LEWIS BLACK

REMEMBER THE BUCOLIC PAINTING that started off the "Marriage" chapter? Full of promise and wonder and harmony? Well, this painting is from that same series, only down the road and down the rabbit hole. One could easily bet that the snark is flying all over the place here.

The irony about divorce these days is that it can kindle long-buried desires . . . to screw your ex[30] with every ounce of anger your bitter heart contains. So sex is still involved, even when you're breaking up. It's everywhere, I'm telling you. The only way to deal with it is to snark. Maybe you'll get a snark-gasm . . .

---

[30] Or his or her lawyer.

lking to gets. ◆ Why do women love cats? Cats are independent, they don't

My husband and I had our best sex during our divorce. It was like cheating on our lawyers.

—PRICILLA LOPEZ

~•~

A lonely divorcee was driving home from work and saw a man hitchhiking. She picked him up, and they started talking.

"What do you do?" she asked him.

"I recently escaped from prison, where I was serving a life sentence for killing my wife."

"Oh, so you're available?"

~•~

Bigamy is having one husband or wife too many. Monogamy is the same.

—OSCAR WILDE

••

Alimony: The ransom that the happy pay to the devil.

—H. L. MENCKEN

•••

Alimony is the screwing you get for the screwing you got.

••

My divorce came to me as a complete surprise. That's what happens when you haven't been home in eighteen years.

—LEE TRAVINO

Things Not to Say During Sex

➤ You're almost as good as my ex!

➤ You look younger than you feel.

➤ Perhaps you're just out of practice.

➤ And to think, I didn't even have to buy you dinner!

➤ I have a confession . . .

➤ I'll tell you whom I'm fantasizing about if you tell me whom you're fantasizing about . . .

➤ Petroleum jelly or no petroleum jelly, I said no.

➤ Keep it down . . . my mother is a light sleeper . . .

➤ My old girlfriend used to do it a *lot* longer!

You mean, apart from my own?
—ZSA ZSA GABOR, WHEN ASKED HOW MANY
HUSBANDS SHE'D HAD

✦✦✦

Nothing is better for the spirit or the body than a love affair.
It elevates thoughts and flattens stomachs.
—BARBARA HOWAR

ome they like to sleep and be left alone. In other words, qualities that women hate

I enjoy dating married people because they never want
anything kinky, like breakfast.
—JONI RODGERS

~✦~

*Q. How do you make your wife scream while
having sex?*
A. Call her and tell her.

~✦~

Adultery is the most conventional way
top rise above the unconventional.
—VLADIMIR NABOKOV

✦✦

A man can have two, maybe three, affairs while
he's married. After that, you're cheating.
—YVES MONTAND

✦✦✦

There are times not to flirt. When you're sick. When you're
with children. When you're on the witness stand.
—JOYCE JILLSON

✦✦

Thou shalt not commit adultery . . . unless in the mood.
—W. C. FIELDS

✦✦✦

I ran into my ex today . . . put it in reverse and did it again.

I'm an excellent housekeeper. Every time
I get divorced, I keep the house.
—ZSA ZSA GABOR

••

I know many married men, I even know a few happily
married men, but I don't know one who wouldn't fall
down the first open manhole running after the first pretty
girl who gives him a wink.
—GEORGE JEAN NATHAN

•••

A sure sign that a man is going to be unfaithful
is if he has a penis.
—JO BRAND

~•~

*A man and his young wife were in divorce
court, but the custody of their children posed a
problem. The mother gets up and says to the
judge that since she brought the children into
this world, she should retain custody of them.
The man also wanted custody of his children,
so the judge asked for his justification. After a
long silence, the man slowly rose from his chair
and replied, "Your Honor, when I put a dollar
in a vending machine and a Coke comes out,
does the Coke belong to me or the machine?"*

~•~

out three inches. • Looking for true love, settling for cheap sex. • My wife and

Snarkin' the Facts

> ➤ Outside of the bedroom, the most common place for adults in the United States to have sex is the car. Hence the reason the stick shift will be a thing of the past.

> ➤ Statistics suggest that approximately one in every five Americans has indulged in sex with a colleague at work. Boy, that person gets around.

> ➤ Viagra, the well-known blue pill designed to help with erectile dysfunction, made $411 million in profits within the first three months of its release in 1998 before going on to make $1.8 billion in 2003. And it's just going to keep going up and up. And staying up.

> ➤ Having sex can make a woman look younger and more attractive. Leaving the lights off more than triples those odds.

> ➤ The typical person spends about six hundred hours having sex between the ages of twenty and seventy. (So if your husband or wife disappears for twenty-five days, you know what they're doing.)

I have the secret to making a marriage last. Two times a week, we go to a nic

Signs that your lover is bored:

➤ Passionless kisses

➤ Frequent sighing

➤ Moved, left no forwarding address

—MATT GROENING

My wife stopped pretending to have orgasms years ago.
That's all right with me, though, because it allowed me to
stop pretending that I cared.
—MIKE RANSTON

✦✦

My wife used to love to talk to me during sex. The other day
she called me from a motel.
—RODNEY DAINGERFIELD

✦✦✦

I once knew a woman who offered her honor
So I honored her offer
And all night long I was on her and off her.

Seven Kinds of Sex

- SMURF SEX—The first throes of passion, when you're fucking until you're blue in the face.

- KITCHEN SEX—You're definitely a couple, but you're still attracted enough to be overcome with desire while making dinner.

- BEDROOM SEX—Her thong has become a brief, he's wearing pajamas, and you usually have sex in bed.

- RELIGIOUS SEX—Nun in the morning, nun in the afternoon, and nun at night.

- HALLWAY SEX—You've been together too long. When you pass each other in the hallway, you say fuck you.

- COURTROOM SEX—Your soon-to-be ex-wife and her lawyer screw you in the divorce court in front of many people and for every penny you've got.

- SOCIAL SECURITY SEX—Back in the game, you now get a little each month. But it's not enough to live on.

will buy anything marked down. Last year she bought an escalator. ✦ Bumper

I just broke up with someone, and the last thing she said to me was, "You'll never find anyone like me again!" I'm thinking, *I should hope not! If I don't want you, why would I want someone like you?*

—KEITH SWEAT

··

When people say, "You're breaking my heart," more often than not, they mean, "You're breaking my balls."

—JEFFREY BERNARD

~·~

Reason for divorce #1: you go to the Hallmark store and ask, "Can you show me to the 'controlling bitch' section?"

Reason for divorce #2: You find an invoice in your spouse's dresser drawer for a hitman.

~·~

I don't see any reason for marriage when there is divorce.

—CATHERINE DENEUVE

··

I hardly said a word to my wife until I said "yes" to divorce.

—JOHN MILIUS

···

I swear, if you existed I'd divorce you.

—EDWARD ALBEE

Roseanne Barr

➤ You may marry the man of your dreams, but fourteen years later, you're married to a couch that burps.

➤ Men read maps better than women because men can understand the concept of an inch equaling a hundred miles.

➤ There are men who like to dress up as women, and when they do, they can no longer parallel park.

➤ The fastest way to a man's heart is through his chest.

➤ I'm only upset that I'm not a widow.
(on her divorce from Tom Arnold)

A bachelor never quite gets over the idea that he is a thing of beauty and a boy forever.
—HELEN ROWLAND

✦✦✦

Love makes the time pass. Time makes love pass.

~✦~

During a routine search, a stowaway girl was discovered by the captain. "What are you doing here?" the Captain asked. "I have an arrangement with one of the sailors," she explained. "I get to go to Europe because he's screwing me." "In more ways than one, lady," said the captain. "This is the Staten Island Ferry."

~✦~

True or False?

➤ "Vagina" is a medical term used to describe heart trouble.

➤ Anus is the Latin word for "yearly."

➤ A diaphragm is a drawing in geometry.

➤ An enema is someone who is not your friend.

Love is the self-delusion we manufacture to justify the trouble we take to have sex.
—DANIEL S. GREENBERG

ircumstances should he be allowed to breed. ✦ I started out to be a sex fiend, but

Why do Jewish divorces cost so much? They're worth it.
—HENNY YOUNGMAN

+++

I don't think I'll get married again. I'll just find a woman I
don't like and buy her a house.
—LEWIS GRIZZARD

++

We would have broken up except for the children. Who
were the children? Well, she and I were.
—MORT SAHL

~+~

*Heinrich Heine left his entire estate to his wife
on the condition she marry again, because,
according to Heine, "There will be a least one
man who will regret my death."*

~+~

What scares me about divorce is my children might put me
in a home for unwed mothers.
—TERESSA SKELTON

+++

You don't know a woman till you've met her in court.
—NORMAN MAILER

I couldn't pass the physical. • Women don't blink during foreplay because there isn

When two people are under the influence of the most violent, most insane, most delusive, and most transient of passions, they are required to swear that they will remain in that excited, abnormal, and exhausting condition continuously until death do them part.
—GEORGE BERNARD SHAW

♦♦

Love is a grave mental disease.
—PLATO

legs. ◆ I have standards. They just happen to be lower than everyone else's. ◆ H

And in Conclusion

AND SO, WE COME to the end. I feel pretty good. Wish I smoked, if only because I love a good cliché. I leave you with these thoughts, dear reader:

Sex will outlive us all.
—SAMUEL GOLDWYN

✦✦✦

Nothing risqué, nothing gained.
—ALEXANDER WOOLCOTT

✦✦

Of all the worldly passions, lust is the most intense. All the other worldly passions seem to follow in its train.
—BUDDHA

THANKS

I OWE THANKS TO A great many people who helped and supported me during the writing of this book.

My deepest thanks go to my editor, Ann, for her great attention to every detail and the care she puts into every project. It was painstaking—I was a pain and she refrained from driving a stake through my heart.

Thanks also to the folks who were always willing to listen, read, put up with, hear out, react and criticize (constructively, of course): Mom, Kevin Lynch, James Naccarato, Karen Patterson, Mark Mirando, the Owl-tards, and everyone at GPP.

Thanks to the all the folks at Skyhorse—Tony, Bill, Esther, Abigail, and the gang.

Finally, thanks to Rosalind—my best friend, lover, heart, soul, and one of the sexiest people on earth.

Index

Adams, John Quincy, 100

Aerosmith, 117

Aesop, 33

Albee, Edward, 153

Allen, Woody, v, 34, 57

Andretti, Mario, 123

Anonymous, 14, 34

Arrested Development, 55, 66, 95

Astor, Nancy, 48

Attel, Dave, 124

Augustine (Saint), 103

Baldwin, Alec, 54

Baldwin, James, 35

Bankhead, Tallulah, 61, 65

Barr, Roseanne, 9, 154

Barry, Dave, 35

Beecham, Sir Thomas, 81

Berlusconi, Silvio, 110

Bernard, Jeffrey, 153

Bierce, Ambrose, 14

Binder, Mike, 4

Bisonette, David, 11

Black, Lewis, 85, 145

Bleeth, Yasmine, 71

Bokor, Daniel, 82

Bombeck, Erma, 42, 107

Boosler, Elayne, 99, 131

Brand, Jo, 48, 149

Braxton, Toni, 91

Brecht, Bertolt, 32

Brown, Larry, 90

Brown, Rita Mae, 77

Buddha, 159

Bukowski, Charles, 34, 37

Burchill, Julie, 143

Burns, Frank (*M.A.S.H.*), 15

Burns, George, 55, 67, 73

Bush, Barbara, 98

Caan, James, 61

Californication, 69, 71

Campbell, Florence, 127

Carlin, George, 15, 81

Carlyle, Cathy, 26

Carr, Coach, *Mean Girls*, 58

Carson, Johnny, 16, 66

Carter, Judy, 103

Carter, Lillian, 103

Chamberlain, Wilt, 121

Chandler, Raymond, 32, 35

Chanel, Coco, 136

Cher, 17

Chesterfield, Lord, 105

Cho, Margaret, 86, 91

Churchill, Winston, 94

Clay, Andrew Dice, 82

Clinton, Kate, 76

Coffey, Paul, 123

Coleridge, Samuel Taylor, 117

Comfort, Alex, 38

Corey, Irwin, 9

Cosby, Bill, 58, 134

Cotter, Tom, 83

Crisp, Quentin, 33, 36

Dangerfield, Rodney, 24, 58, 65, 67, 151

Davidson, Brenda, 17

Davis, Bette, 15, 73

Dedopulos, Tim, 37

Delaria, Lea, 77

Democratus, 42

Deneuve, Catherine, 153

Dietrich, Marlene, 55

Diller, Phyllis, 71, 89

Disraeli, Benjamin, 10

Dobbin, John, 135-6

Duc D'Aumale, Henri, 40

Duchess of Windsor, The, 105

Duck Soup, 58

Dumas, Alexandre, 14

Durst, Will, 90, 97

Dury, Ian, 89
Dykes, Sandra J., 134
Eastwood, Clint, 19
Egan, Cecilia, 51
Eliot, George, 11
Ellison, Harlan, 43
Ephron, Nora, 39
Erasmus, Desiderius, 32
Faldo, Nich, 21
Falwell, Jerry, 101
Fara, George, 124
Feiffer, Jules, 103
Fields, W. C., 56, 63, 148
Fox, Megan, 61
Foxworthy, Jeff, 4, 20
Foxx, Redd, 71
Franklin, Benjamin, 109
Frasier, 63
Friedman, Bruce Jay, 39
Gable, Clark, 63
Gabor, Zsa Zsa, 4, 21, 58, 147, 149
Galas, Diamanda, 101
Gardner, Ava, 80
George, David Lloyd, 36

Giamatti, A. Bartlett, 124
Gizzard, Lewis, 5, 36, 39, 156
Goldberg, Isaac, 32
Goldfinger, 62
Goldsmith, Warren H., 116
Goldwyn, Samuel, 159
Gottfried, Gilbert, 39
Greenberg, Daniel S., 155
Greer, Germaine, 51
Groening, Matt, 61, 70, 151
Guccione, Bob, 39
Gusoff, Adrienne, 137-8
Hall, Rich, 82
Handey, Jack, 19
Handler, Chelsea, 80, 86
Harshman, Marv, 124
Hedberg, Mitch, 46
Heimel, Cynthia, 100, 128
Hepburn, Katharine, 51
Herbert, Allan Patrick, 20
Hicks, Bill, 41, 110
Hill, Dave, 126
Hoffenstein, Samuel, 99
Hollander, Xaviera, 131

Homer, 41

House, 73

Hower, Barbara, 147

Hull, Raymond, 11

Humphries, Barry, 142

Hornung, Paul, 5

Irwin, Hale, 123

Jackson, Glenda, 60

Jackson, Reggie, 121

James, Ray, 125

Jeremy, Ron, 68

Jillson, Joyce, 148

Joel, Billy, 81

Johnson, Samuel, 22

Jong, Erica, 50, 77

Joplin, Janice, 83

Jung, Carl, 38

Kauffman, Max, 7

Kelly, Bill, 95

Kimmel, Jimmy, 71

Kindler, Andy, 89

Knightley, Kiera, 62

Knocked Up, 61

Korman, Harvey, 136

L.A. Story, 55

Lampanelli, Lisa, 128

Lavner, Lynn, 108

Lawrence, D. H., 30

Leary, Denis, 91

Lebowitz, Fran, 19, 27, 31, 45

Lette, Kathy, 50

Letterman, David, 68

Lewis, C. S., 42

Lewis, Richard, 86, 98, 137

Liefer, Carol, 76

Lien, Jon, 138

Lincoln, Abraham, 108

Lombardi, Vince, 123

Lopez, Priscilla, 146

Machamar, Jefferson, 14

Madonna, 81, 87, 92

Maher, Bill, 19, 87

Mailer, Norman, 156

Manning, Bernard, 94

Mansfield, Jayne, 17

Maron, Marc, 83

Martin, Steve, 39

Marx, Groucho, 60, 73, 112, 114

Marx, Karl, 109
Mason, Jackie, 79
Maugham, W. Somerset,
    22, 27, 32
McFadden, Reggie, 85
McLaughlin, Mignon, 10
Mencken, Henry Louis, v,
    4, 146
Milholland, Randy K., 42
Milius, John, 153
Miller, Dennis, 68
Monkhouse, Bob, 14
Montad, Yves, 148
Moore, Christopher, 46, 117
Moore, Dudley, 91, 117
Morgan, Robin, 30
Morrow, Lance, 30
Mortimer, John, 35
Nabokov, Vladimir, 148
Nash, Ogden, 17, 29
Nathan, George Jean, 149
Nelms, Cynthia, 132
Nielsen, Leslie, 120
Nietzsche, Friedrich, 10,
    115, 116

O'Brien, Conan, 69
O'Rourke, P. J., 5
Ogilvie, O. C., 11
Onassis, Jacqueline
    Kennedy, 98
Orwell, George, 122
Osberg, Brad, 18
Paglia, Camille, 33, 76
Paley, Maggie, 136-7
Palmer, Arnold, 122
Parker, Dorothy, 31, 42
Perelman, S. J., 80
Peters, Russell, 135
Philips, Emo, 91, 132
Piaf, Edith, 83
Plato, 157
Pretty Woman, 55
Private Benjamin, 59
Pryor, Richard, 85
Raleigh, Sir Walter, 21
Ranston, Mike, 151
Reed, Jerry, 80
Rivers, Joan, 5, 54, 66, 71
Roberts, Shelley, 77
Rodgers, Joni, 148

Rodman, Dennis, 121
Roeben, Scott, 34, 114, 133
Rooney, Andy, 66
Rose, Don, 134
Ross, Stanely Ralph, 109
Rowland, Helen, 4, 20, 154
Rozzi, Giulia, 121
Rudner, Rita, 7, 21, 91
Runckle, Marcy, 3
Russell, Bertrand, 15
deSade, Marquis, 30
Sagan, Francoise, 114
Sahl, Mort, 156
Samantha, *Sex and the City*, 56, 58
Sayer, Dorothy L., 10
Schrader, Don, 103
Schumer, Amy, 81
Sedaris, Amy, 82
Sedaris, David, 95
Seinfeld, 59, 67
Sex and the City, 67
Shakespeare, William, 43-5
Shandling, Garry, 59, 67, 72, 83, 90, 133

Shaw, George Bernard, 10, 157
Shriner, Will, 115
Silverman, Sarah, 80, 87
Simon, Neil, 31
Skelton, Teressa, 156
Slayton, Bobby, 7
Snow, Carrie, 108
Socrates, 27
Sokol, Marilyn, 17
Spear, Geoff, 132
Spiro, Lev L., 56
Steinem, Gloria, 100
Stern, Howard, 69
Stoppard, Tom, 92
Superbad, 59
Susskind, Carol, 48, 142
Sweat, Keith, 153
Talmud, The, 109
Tennyson, Alfred Lord, 32
Tenuta, Judy, 128
Thompson, Hunter S., 45
Tomlin, Lily, 49, 107
Travino, Lee, 146
Turner, Tina, 87

Twain, Mark, 41, 107
Updike, John, 34
Ustinov, Peter, 34
Van Horn, William, 123
Vidal, Gore, 35, 100, 116
Voltaire, 41, 101
Ward, William A., 123
Warhol, Andy, 53
Waters, John, 100
Watson, Thomas, 122
Waugh, Evelyn, 33
West, Mae, 70
West, Rebecca, 51

Wharton, Edith, 20
Wilde, Oscar, 30, 41, 146
Williams, Danny, 130
Williams, Harlan, 85
Williams, Robin, 86, 92
Wooden, John, 122
Woolcott, Alexander, 159
Wright, Steven, 86
Yaghmour, Feras, 143
Youngman, Henny, 156
Yori, Myers, 39
Zappa, Frank, 80